SOUL SALVATION
A GEN X LOVE LETTER TO THE ENGLISH BEAT
By Marc Wasserman

First published in August 2024

by DiWulf Publishing

Morrisville, Pennsylvania

diwulf.com

Printed in the United States of America

ISBN: 979-8-9900264-2-1

Table of Contents

Soul Salvation

Dedication

This book is dedicated to the memory of my mother Jill Hinden Wasserman. Thank you for teaching me to love reading books and for being there when I needed you most.

Soul Salvation

Foreword

I was still in college when I co-founded I.R.S. Records in 1979 with Miles Copeland who was then the manager of The Police. Little did we know that by the late 1980s, the small label we had started from scratch would become one of the most prominent independent music labels in North America. From humble beginnings and hard work we ended up launching the careers of R.E.M., the Go-Go's, Wall Of Voodoo and the English Beat, who would all go on to create the foundation for the modern rock radio format that took off in the 1990s.

While I loved all the bands we signed to the label, the English Beat always held a special place in my heart. When we signed them in 1982 ahead of the release of the Special Beat Service album, it was a huge turning point for us as a label and I was certain we could make them successful in America. And we came very close.

I first heard the English Beat's debut 1979 single "Tears of A Clown," and was captivated. Though they were initially tagged as part of the vibrant British 2 Tone ska and reggae scene, I found their music to be both more mainstream and more complex than their contemporaries. Their songs were driven by the extraordinary bass lines of David "Shuffle" Steele and the drumming of Everett Morton that meshed with the sharp pop sensibilities of Dave

Wakeling and the melodic guitar playing of Andy Cox. Add in the colorful and charismatic toasting of Ranking Roger and the iconic sax lines of Saxa and you had a sound that was truly unique, danceable and marketable.

The band were a collection of very different personalities which was both their strength and their challenge:

- Dave Wakeling was prickly back in the day; alternately charming and combative; I think he was very ambitious yet insecure, and frightened that it was all not going to work out.
- Ranking Roger was warm and friendly always; that big smile greeting you every time you met.
- Andy and Shuffle were quiet, but they were sharp intellects who missed nothing. When they chose to speak it was thoughtful and important to them.

What we didn't know as we prepared to release Special Beat Service in the fall of 1982 was that the end was near. Nevertheless, we worked hard to find innovative and unique ways to promote the band and build on the rabid cult following they had developed through constant touring. Both "Save It For Later" and "I Confess" were songs that we thought would connect with music programmers and listeners and we produced striking videos for both songs that garnered MTV airplay that introduced them to an even bigger American audience. And when "Save It For Later" cracked the Billboard Top 40 we celebrated! We were the small indie label that could!

One of my strongest memories of the band and of their potential was when they captivated more than 150,000 fans at the second US Festival in May of 1983 at the tail end of their Special Beat Service tour of North America. The band gave heartfelt shoutouts to our small team of passionate music champions at the label (a very rare thing for bands to do from the stage) and we all knew this band was well on the way to being superstars.

But then just a few weeks later, after the band returned home to Birmingham and played three sold out shows with David Bowie, we got the news that the English Beat were done. The message that "we are breaking up the band" simply did not compute; they were a rocket ship that had made it through the atmosphere and were just starting their ride to stardom. But it just wasn't meant to be... Though we were shocked and saddened by the unexpected end of the band, I.R.S. did end up signing both General Public and Fine Young Cannibals, whose success was built on the musical DNA of the English Beat and the hard work of our label.

As a live band the English Beat had few peers when it came to their ability to create a party and put joy on the faces of their audience who couldn't stand still once the music started. In all the nights I dragged a radio programmer or music journalist to see an English Beat show, I never once had the evening end without my guest gushing "they are an incredible live band."

Original and innovative are terms music people toss around too much when describing artists, but in the case of the English Beat, both terms are true. They truly sounded like no one else. Their songwriting and musicianship were top shelf. And now forty years later we are finally acknowledging their important musical contribution and lasting legacy.

Enjoy Marc's loving look back at a band who really made a difference to him and all of us.

Jay Boberg
Co-founder of I.R.S Records (1979-1993)
July 2024

Introduction

"Every story has to be about something, I suppose…"

-Doors Of Your Heart

Marc backstage with Dave Wakeling at the Sellersville Theatre in 2006

I immediately recognized Dave Wakeling standing alone outside the Canal Room. He was smoking a cigarette, lost in his own thoughts. Now in his early 50s, he looked remarkably young, healthy, and vibrant. His chiseled matinee idol face features soft eyes, an inviting smile that was topped off by a full head of blonde hair. In fact, he looked exactly the way he was described by the band's bassist David Steele the first time he met him on the Isle of Wight in 1978: "*some kind of grapefruit salesman.*"[i] And while

Steele may have said that in jest, I meant it in the best way possible.

It was a cold night in mid-January 2006 and my band Bigger Thomas – the first ska and reggae band from New Jersey -- had been hand-picked by Wakeling, sight unseen, to open two shows for his American version of the English Beat. The Canal Room was located on a busy corner of Manhattan near the entrance to the Holland Tunnel in Tribeca and it was well known for booking '80s legacy bands that fill its 450+ capacity space. Though Wakeling was the only original member of a band now made up of LA-based studio musicians, the lure of hearing the band's songs sung by one of its original front men remained a strong draw.

In the pre-social media days of the early 2000s, Wakeling was accessible to fans on the band's very active website message board. When looking for a support act for his two-night tour stop in New York, he posted a question asking for recommendations for openers. I saw the post and casually responded by mentioning that my band, Bigger Thomas, would be a good choice. I then promptly forgot all about it. Then, a few weeks before Christmas, while scanning the back pages of *The Village Voice*, I spied an ad for the Canal Room listing us as the opener for two shows with the English Beat!

I was flabbergasted, and it took a few minutes for the news to sink in. It seemed like the music gods had finally heard my prayers and presented me with an opportunity I had fantasized about for years.

I'd co-founded Bigger Thomas at Rutgers University in the summer of 1988. The band quickly charmed New Brunswick, New Jersey — a thriving college music town -- and then we'd become part of the early wave of late 80s American ska bands formed in the wake of 2 Tone bands like the English Beat, the Specials, the Selecter, and Madness. As such, my bandmates and I witnessed the birth of a uniquely American version of ska that mixed new wave, punk, metal, and hardcore. But our main influences were drawn from the 2 Tone bands and the English Beat in particular.

As I approached Wakeling, he glanced up, took a drag on his cigarette and blew a big puff of smoke up above my head as he offered me a warm, welcoming smile. I introduced myself, and he was immediately complimentary about the band and our sound, saying: "I think you will be a good combination with the Beat." Buzzing from this compliment, I began peppering him with all the questions I'd ever had about the band: what was "Save It For Later" really about? (The tough transition from adolescence to adulthood); did the band really break up after being asked by David Bowie to tour with him? (Yes); did he still speak with Ranking

Roger? (Sometimes); was there any chance the band would ever get back together? (You never know!).

Though he'd likely been asked these questions thousands of times before, he good-naturedly answered each one of mine, like it was the very first time he'd ever heard them. It was clear that Wakeling had perfected the instant familiarity of speaking with strangers, likely honed over years of touring and countless interviews. Like those lucky few who are blessed with charm, Wakeling quickly put me at ease, making me feel as if we'd known each other for years rather than mere minutes.

Before I realized it, half an hour had passed, and I was still standing alone next to one of my musical heroes, a person whose songs helped shape me into the musician and the human being I had become. Suddenly a side door opened and a soundman stuck his head out looking for Wakeling. Upon seeing him he announced, "It's time for soundcheck." Wakeling looked at me, shook my hand and said, "See you in there," and made his way inside. I stood alone outside on the street in a state of shock, trying to process our conversation and kicking myself for all the questions I hadn't asked him.

The two nights at the Canal Room were a blur of nervous energy and anticipation. The club was packed with a mix of young, local

New York City ska fans and a boisterous crowd of suburban 40- and 50-somethings who had travelled in from the suburbs of Long Island and New Jersey to hear songs from their youth. Being on stage in front of a big crowd is one of the most exhilarating experiences in life, and when the crowd is with you it's hard to describe the effect it had on your serotonin levels. Both nights my bandmates and I rose to the occasion and played our best 40-minute set, impressing the crowd (who cheered us on) and Wakeling, who we spied watching us from the side of the stage.

Once we finished our opening band duties, I took up a spot in the back of the club near the sound booth to watch Wakeling and his band perform. It was the first time I'd seen him play live since a warm spring night at the Jersey Shore in 1983. Back then the visceral experience of seeing the band for the first time meant everything to me. My senses were overwhelmed by the stage lights that blinked in unison to the push and pull of the crowd that undulated in time to the music. I distinctly remember the pungent odor of spilled beer, cigarettes and sweat. It was as much a physical experience as an emotional one. And it stayed with me for years.

Now, into my early 40s, the years rolled back as Wakeling opened his set with "Rough Rider." But this time I had older and wiser musician's ears and I let each song wash over me. As an adult the songs impacted me differently. There was still the same excitement

15

and nervous energy I'd felt as a teen, but now it was more satisfying emotionally than physically. As Wakeling prefaced each song with a pithy introduction, he conjured a mix of emotions in me. The overriding sense I had was of living in the moment and being transported back in time.

After the show, Wakeling gave me his booking agent's name and number and told me to call him for other support slots that Spring. We ended up playing a series of shows across the Northeast with his band which were a great education for us about life on the road. But nothing was more surreal than standing with Wakeling and making small talk while waiting to check in to the same roadside motel.

The truth is that meeting Wakeling remains one of the most important touchstones of my life. And though I'd put him on a pedestal, he was kind and personable in a way I could never have imagined. Despite many trials and tribulations, including falling out with the key members of the original line-up, Wakeling has continued to persevere and perform the band's music for audiences made up of people just like me. We've all grown up together with these songs and the collective experience of hearing them again can be a religious experience.

The quarter century between when I discovered the band and this specific moment in time had been spent playing music inspired by Wakeling and the English Beat. I'd spent thousands of hours listening to the band's records, reading articles about them, and writing music inspired by their sound, but finally meeting Wakeling was the payoff for years of fandom. As Carl Jung wrote: *"Your vision will become clear only when you can look into your own heart. Who looks outside dreams, who looks inside, awakes."* That night in 2006, after years of dreaming, I was finally awake.

Marc Wasserman
July, 2024

Soul Salvation

Preface

"I was never very happy, even as a kid. I was the rebellious type." [ii]

--Dave Wakeling

I wasn't a happy kid either. But rather than the rebellious type, I was the deadly serious type. This fact became abundantly clear to my parents early on. My father found my seriousness so concerning that his earliest advice to me was: "Put Super Glue in your toothpaste and smile more." What he didn't know was that I hated my smile. I had crooked teeth. But, more importantly, I hated being told that I should pretend to be happy. Much to my chagrin, this will be something that people will repeat to me throughout my childhood: *just smile more.* Smiling felt awkward.

Thankfully, '70s pop music – AM radio and then 45 singles – gave me moments of great joy and much-needed relief from the toll that everyday life was taking on my soul. I completely disappeared into the sounds emanating from my parent's car radios and the grooves of black vinyl that undulated hypnotically on their turntable. Gilbert O'Sullivan's "Alone Again (Naturally)" was an obsessive favorite and, even as a child, the line "*In my hour of need I truly am indeed, alone again, naturally*" resonated with me. That lyric was me in a nutshell from ages 8 to 11. I played that song over and over again.

I spent a lot of time alone. But inside my head I lived in colorful fantasy worlds that I created around music. As I listened to my growing collection of LPs and 45 singles, small movies came to life in my mind's eye. As I grew older, certain songs just connected with that hidden part of my soul stimulated by pop music. These songs gave me a warm tingly sensation in my chest and when that happened time stopped, and I absorbed the melody and rhythms with my whole being. I paid particular attention to lyrics. Not just the big choruses but the second and third verses that rounded out the stories being told. Deciphering and memorizing lyrics made me happy even if the song was sad. In fact, the sadder the song or the darker the circumstances, the better. Sad songs stimulated my brain and heart in a way that party songs never did. If a song gave me a lump in my throat, it was a hit with me.

As the '70s gave way to the '80s, the radio offered up a plethora of new sounds – punk, new wave, reggae – with angry and confrontational personal and political lyrics. Soon enough, my serious side morphed to reveal a rebellious side as well. I soon realized I was growing a rather large chip on my shoulder to rival the sizeable lump in my throat from all the sad songs I'd been listening to.

My life was forever altered by a momentous trip to the Philippines with one of my best friends and his family during the summer of 1979. During the month-long trip I came down with a virus that made me very sick. Away from my family for the first time, I was forced, at 14 years of age, to learn fortitude and resilience, and to be brave in the face of intense homesickness, physical pain, and mental anxiety. Upon my return home, transformed by the experience, and very ill and hospitalized, it was clear that everything around me had changed, including music.

In case you weren't there, the dawn of the 80s was unnerving for a kid like me. Between the threat of nuclear war, gas shortages, and the rise of a growing conservative political movement, I innocently held out hope that kindhearted and earnest Jimmy Carter would be re-elected President and that my parents' marriage might withstand the pressures that threatened to cause its collapse. On Tuesday November 4, 1980, I was stunned by the ferocity of the electoral landslide that put Ronald Reagan and the Republican Party into power and slammed by the harsh reality that my parents were quickly barreling towards a permanent separation.

As Reagan was being inaugurated on January 20, 1981, my father was preparing to move out of our family home. I would see him sporadically over the next ten years as he moved around the

country -- from Providence to Minneapolis to Denver and
Cincinnati looking for steady work as a department store buyer.

 It was during this time, when in dire need of some type of musical
catharsis, that the English Beat and their three albums came into
my life in quick succession. Each album: *I Just Can't Stop It,*
Wha'ppen, and *Special Beat Service* mirrored distinct phases of my
adolescence and, as trite as it may sound, I grew in tandem with
each album. I went from being a sad, sickly 15-year-old in 1980 to a
politically aware and angry 16-year-old in 1981 to a burgeoning 17-
year-old new romantic and would-be musician by 1982.

Much of that had to do with the lyrics and music of the English
Beat. I'd argue that Wakeling is a wordsmith on par with Elvis
Costello and Paul Weller and parsing the word play of his lyrics
became an academic sport for me. I loved the ritual and routine of
taking the band's albums out of their sleeves, placing them
reverently on my turntable, and listening while I gazed at the
album covers. I closed my eyes, letting my mind wander as I
listened to Wakeling and Ranking Roger take me on a ride through
an England that, like me, was undergoing massive changes.

While the records helped me through the day-to-day challenges of
my life, it was seeing the English Beat live in 1983, just a few
weeks before they would break up, that was the payoff for years of

musical worship. While all three albums helped to make me the man and the musician I am today, *Special Beat Service* holds a special place in my heart. Its mature themes were as important to me as the range of emotions and human drama I'd been learning about reading the plays and sonnets of William Shakespeare in my 12th grade English class. Wakeling's lyrics looked inside an increasingly dark and complicated world full of inequality, racism, sexism, misunderstanding, anger, and betrayal. At the same time, those songs cultivated ideas about perseverance, forgiveness, tolerance, and acceptance. And for that I am eternally grateful.

I've long felt that it was my destiny to write a book about the band. Much of that sense stems from several twists of fate that put me in touch with almost all the members of the band. And for that reason, I've lovingly and carefully researched the making of *Special Beat Service*. I've re-visited the band's origin story, reviewed their impressions of one another, and researched their hopes and expectations as they prepared to write, record, and release *Special Beat Service* in 1982 and perform songs from it across America during 1982 and 1983.

What's clear is that, at its heart, *Special Beat Service* is an experimental swan song of an album that combines pop, ska, reggae, punk, soul, new wave, and Latin music into twelve unique, stand-alone songs created by a band that was growing exhausted from the grind of trying to break America. And while grappling with the drudgery of constant touring, band members were confronted with a hard truth: they weren't sure they wanted to be in a band with each other anymore. That ambivalence may have contributed to *Special Beat Service's* go-for-broke sound, making it one of the most overlooked albums of the early '80s.

Amazingly, *Special Beat Service* remains an album many critics name check, but haven't really considered, even retrospectively. The fact is that the album features several iconic songs of the era, some of which are the earliest examples of a nascent, early 80s indie rock sound just beginning to find its footing.

Despite fantastic songs and a stunning live show built on several years of constant touring, *Special Beat Service* didn't make the artistic and sales impact it could or should have. As Simon Price passionately wrote about the album in *The Quietus* in 2014:

> *The decline in sales was sharp. Special Beat Service only reached No.23 on its release in 1982. The world wasn't listening. And the world was a sucker because Special Beat Service is a wonderful, wonderful record. Wakeling's songwriting had stepped up a level, mature in the best possible sense (i.e. the sense that isn't just code for 'fucking boring'), his lyrics showing a rare subtlety and depth.*

Straight-up ska-pop numbers like 'Jeanette' and jerky, fidgety punk-funkers like 'Rotating Head' were a throwback to the earlier material, but SBS was dominated by thoughtful songs about relationship break-ups, with the sort of chord changes that reach in, grab your heart in a fist, and twist. On tracks like 'Save It For Later' (which belatedly broke The Beat in America when MTV and college radio picked up on it), with its classic chiming guitars, the ska revival felt like a distant memory. Even jazzy piano breaks were now allowed on 'I Confess' and the astonishingly beautiful 'End Of The Party.' I played it to the point of destruction, in the full knowledge that almost nobody else was. [iii]

Like Price, I also played *Special Beat Service* to the point of destruction. The album arrived just as I was making the transition to young adulthood and it became a ritual for me to put it on and sit and listen to it quietly and respectfully. Sometimes at night. Sometimes in the morning. Sometimes on a cassette tape on a JC Penny knockoff Walkman while riding my bike. The lyrics soothed me and the music that accompanied them became so entrenched in my memory that distinct phrases from songs would float in and out of my consciousness at the oddest times. I listened so often and memorized the album tracking to such an extent that I could anticipate the first notes of the next song just as the previous song ended. The lyrics became a type of prayer and meditation. I would recite them in my mind or quietly mouth them to myself. And, as I did, I would imagine what it would be like to write songs that might move others the way these songs moved me. My desire for an intimate connection to and through music was so intense that I invented fake bands with logos and fake song titles.

And, for many years, I felt like I might be one of the few fans who carried a flame for the *Special Beat Service*. Later, others who shared my passion made it more widely known. In a retrospective review of the album for *Rolling Stone* Jody Rosen wrote:

> *...although ska was always the bedrock of their sound, they were really just a pop band, led by a great singer-songwriter, Dave Wakeling – for my money, the* ne plus ultra *of whimpery British white boys. My favorite is the band's studio album,* Special Beat Service *(1983). Songs like 'Sole Salvation,' 'End of the Party,' and 'I Confess' are as catchy and as savagely witty as anything by Elvis Costello, and Wakeling is far less impressed with his own smarts than Costello.* [iv]

Certainly, one of the album's greatest creative triumphs remains "Save It For Later," whose cultural impact may be that it has been covered by two icons of rock music: Pete Townshend of the Who and

Eddie Vedder of Pearl Jam. Amazingly, it's a song the band – then in the process of disintegrating -- wasn't in full agreement about recording. Members had to be pushed and cajoled by I.R.S. Records to record it.

"Save It For Later" turned out to be a minor U.S. hit, but the Velvet Underground drone meets the Byrds-like chime of it was miles away from the band's original, angsty, punky reggae roots. But the album's new, experimental sound showed creative growth, and when joined to lyrics that slyly allude to oral sex ("Save It For Later"), the suspicions and paranoia of secret service agents ("Rotating Heads"), and the ruminations of a sociopathic cheater who realizes too late he's also done himself fatal, emotional harm ("I Confess"), say something profound about the push and pull of the creative process. It also illuminates the ways that bands can come together creatively, or, in the case of the English Beat, come together creatively in the act of falling apart. And, despite clear signals that the band had run its course, Wakeling urged himself and his bandmates on with the poignant lyrics in "Sole Salvation," offering: *"There's a new dance, the tolerance, and it just might be your sole salvation."*

Though the band couldn't hold their marriage of diverse musical influences together, *Special Beat Service* is historically important for capping off the initial 2 Tone ska revival, and for ushering in other notable early 80s new wave sounds that incorporated elements of reggae, R&B and soul (see Elvis Costello, the Jam, the Clash, Joe Jackson). In that sense, *Special Beat Service* can be seen as an important transitional album in the context of its specific musical era. Four-plus decades after its release in 1982, I believe it deserves love and respect. And now that several original members of the band have passed on, I feel a particular urgency to document how much *Special Beat Service* means to me and to so many others.

My homage to *Special Beat Service* intertwines with my own personal experiences during this critical time period, and I reflect on how the band and the album served as a totem for me, one that helped me endure trying and difficult times. And while it may be hyperbolic, I think it helped to save my life or at the very least to put me on a specific path. And, like my father did years earlier, it urged me on through the lyrics of "Ackee 1-2-3" to smile through it all:

> *Someone just smiled*
> *for no special reason,*
> *It looks like the smile's*
> *come back into season*
> *It's so easy*
> *It doesn't have to be a nice day,*
> *Just the only one you've got*
> *And it's coming ready or not!*
> *Ackee 1 2 3*
> *Ackee 1 2 1 2 3*

September 18, 1982

"We're goin' hoppin', we're goin' hoppin' today, where things are poppin' the Philadelphia way..."

--American Bandstand Theme Song

It's Saturday, September 18, 1982, and I am patiently awaiting the arrival of *American Bandstand*. I'm slouched in front of a Panasonic black and white TV in my small bedroom, located on the second floor of a split-level house on a quiet suburban street in Princeton, New Jersey.

The *TV Guide* listing for today's episode of *American Bandstand* reads: "*The English Beat perform "Save It for Later" & "Sugar and Stress." Men at Work perform "Who Can It Be Now?" & "Down Under"*ᵛ

As music and the English Beat have become an obsession, I've developed a distinct Saturday morning ritual. First I'd read (or reread) the latest issues of *Trouser Press* and *Rolling Stone;* then I'd tune in to watch Dick Clark, host of *American Bandstand*. Dubbed "America's Oldest Teenager," Clark was roughly the same age as my parents, but much cooler. Unlike my parents, Clark and I like the same music. Over the two years I've been a devoted watcher of the show, he's booked many of the bands I love: A Flock Of Seagulls, Squeeze, Devo, Haircut 100, Simple Minds, the Go-Go's, Public Image, ABC, Talking Heads, Berlin, Adam & the Ants, and now, the English Beat.

At the time, Princeton was still a few years off from being wired for cable, so MTV and an endless stream of music videos remained an elusive dream. Until then, it's *American Bandstand*. And that was fine with me. I liked the pace of the show, I loved the Rate-A-Record segment and though I would never admit it to anyone, I enjoyed watching all the smiling, attractive California teens who dressed and danced better than I could ever imagine.

I was 11 years old when we returned to Princeton during the summer of 1976. After three years in the Boston suburb of Medfield where we moved in 1973, the growing hairline fissures in my parents' marriage have become a series of compound fractures. After my father lost another job in the spring of 1976, my mother insisted that we move back to Princeton, and we end up buying a house just two blocks from where we had previously lived.

I'm initially relieved to be back in a place that feels familiar. On the outside it seems like things may be getting back to normal. My father has recently started a new job as a jewelry buyer for the discount department store Jamesway, and my mother, buoyed by being back in Princeton, has started working again. Her first job is in the housewares department of the local Bamberger's department store in the Princeton Shopping Center, where she demonstrates how to cook Chinese food with a wok – then still a novelty for most Americans. I'd often meet her there after school while she stir-fried vegetables for curious customers. After a quick hello she would send me off to the Music Cellar, a record store a few doors down from the Bamberger's, with a few dollars to buy a 45.

With our parents working out of the house every weekday, my younger sister Wendy and I looked after ourselves. Once school let out for the day, I'd ride my bike home and meet Wendy, who is three years younger than me. Our afternoons consisted of making snacks, doing homework, arguing, listening to music, arguing, and watching TV. Lots of TV.

Like many Generation X kids, the specter of divorce had threatened our family for some time. My parents could just not get along and argued often. After dinner they would each go to separate rooms in the house and spend their evenings apart. This went on for several years, until just days before I turned 16 in

January of 1981. My parents separated, and my father moved out to a semi-furnished apartment a few towns away. We saw him infrequently after that. As a result, 1981 was the start of a new, more complicated life for all of us.

Once I turned 17 years old, the sounds of new wave music began to dominate my listening habits. I saved money from doing odd jobs in my neighborhood and began visiting the Music Cellar a few days a week to peruse records and singles. As I slowly accumulated a record collection, I developed rituals for when and how I listened to them. Often at night, before going to sleep, I'd turn off the lights in my room, plug in my headphones, lay down on the floor and listen to one or two albums from start to finish. On weekends, I planned out two- and three-hour listening sessions. At the time, it seemed like a way to escape from reality, but I know now that I was getting an informal musical education. And American Bandstand was an important part of that education.

The English Beat had travelled thousands of literal and figurative miles for this *American Bandstand* performance. It had been three and a half years since they made their debut at The Matador pub in

Birmingham, England on March 31, 1979. Then a four-piece featuring Wakeling and Andy Cox on guitars, Steele on bass and Everett Morton on drums, the band still needed an official name just days before their first show. Malu Halasa (who later married Cox) explained how the band selected their moniker in her band origin story book *Twist & Crawl*:

> *Two days before the gig, Dave began thinking that their combo should have a name. Picking up a Roget's Thesaurus, he looked up the entry for 'harmony;' under that he found 'beat.' The thesaurus also mentioned that the opposite of 'beat' was 'clash' and 'discordant.' 'Hmm, that sounds about right,' he told the lads, who thought 'beat' needed another word with it. Suggestions like 'the Automo-Beat' didn't sound right, so in the end 'The Beat' would just have to do.*[vi]

The newly christened band's first show was opening for a noisy punk band featuring a charismatic 16-year-old Black punk vocalist and drummer with dyed blonde hair named Ranking Roger. He remembered the first gig:

> *When I first met the Beat, I was in a punk band called the Dum Dum Boys and I was their drummer. This band called the Beat wanted to open for us at a gig at a place called The Matador in The Bull Ring. They came to a rehearsal, played*

'Twist & Crawl' and 'Mirror in the Bathroom' and I thought, 'We've got some work to do.' We did the gig; they came on and the place went mad. We knew then that the Beat had won the day. They started wanting me to come to their gigs to check them out. They were playing a place in town called the Mercat Cross, so I went down there and there were six people in there. I said, 'Do you want me to get some people?' and they were like, 'Yeah, we're on in half an hour.' So, I ran down a quarter of a mile to The Crown pub, where all the punks hung out on Hill Street. It was a Wednesday night and some of them were bored out of their heads, some sniffing glue and some of them were just drunk. I said, 'Remember that band the Beat that opened for us? They're playing down this place, the Mercat Cross.

"Now, there must have been about 150 punks following me to this place. I remember the police cars, the Black Marias coming past, and it looked like we were going on a rampage to look for trouble. But we weren't, we were all talking – 'This is gonna be exciting." It better be Rog or we're gonna get ya! We got into this place, and it filled out all of a sudden and then the band went on. I got shoved on the stage, so I picked up the mic and started toasting and they all started going mad. I came off and about two numbers later again they pushed me back on and the band didn't mind. vii

The Beat was started by school friends Wakeling and Cox, who came from the multi-racial Birmingham neighborhoods of Balsall Heath and Handsworth respectively. Growing up in Balsall Heath, Wakeling had been exposed to reggae and ska. As a passionate supporter of the Aston Villa football club, he heard ska, rocksteady, and early reggae played at matches all across Birmingham:

> *It came sideways at me from the football terraces in Birmingham. At Villa and the Blues you'd mainly hear the Trojan albums Tighten Up volumes 1 through 4. And West Bromwich played The Liquidator before the start of each game to stop the skinheads hitting each other.* [viii]

A profile in *The Face* from 1981 explained that Wakeling and Cox had met at a further education college – a school designed to equip students with job-specific skills transferable into the workplace, thus boosting their employability. The pair soon began writing songs together:

> *Quiet Andy reckons he was a 'model scholar,' but he was elbowed towards a further education college to complete his English and history A-levels because his hair was too long. He's 25 now, so this was happening before educationalists discovered that short hair is subversive too and, in fact, that children are entirely the wrong sort of people to be going to*

school. But. . . his mum had bought him a guitar when he
was 14 and 'I've been battering away at it ever since.'

Garrulous Dave is not the sort of person to carry a chip on
his shoulder and yet his school could have given him one:
'King Edward, it was very middle-class, half state and half
foundation.' The question seemed to be whether you were
going to start training as a doctor or merchant banker before
or after university.

Not quite Dave's league. His father was unemployed,
anxiously so, for much of this time. Dave enjoyed sports,
didn't do his homework and expanded his mind by means
literary and chemical: 'We had a liberal headmaster and so
we were introduced at perhaps a too tender age to. . . well,
Carlos Castaneda in the third form.' Setting aside his
father's advice to seek his niche in the RAF or the motor
trade, Dave got together with Andy at college and after. [ix]

Wakeling and Cox had worked out some Van Morrison and Tim
Buckley songs, and it was during these early songwriting sessions
that Cox noticed Wakeling was playing his guitar upside down:

> *It wasn't until I got to 17 that I realised I was playing it*
> *wrong when I met Andrew. We started to play together. He*

said, 'Er... you're holding it upside down.' 'Oh' I said. 'Shit!' I didn't realise you had to change the strings over if you wanted to hold it that way. It's good, though, because you can play chords that nobody else can. ˣ

Wakeling's youthful experimentation with his upside-down guitar would yield considerable results later.

During this time, Cox's American brother-in-law offered them an opportunity to work for him building solar panels at a site on the Isle of Wight. By the time the duo relocated from the urban decay of inner-city Birmingham to bucolic Blackgang Chine on the southern tip of the Isle of Wight, they were composing their own original songs. By 1977, the seeds of the Beat and an embryonic version of their eclectic sonic palette was beginning to blossom in a cottage they shared with a close friend named Marilyn Hebrides. Hebrides would later be put in charge of the band's fan club and newsletter, *The Noise In This World*.

I was on the Isle of Wight sharing a cottage with a few friends (including Dave Wakeling and Andy Cox) while we were building some solar panels. I remember Dave hogging the bathroom all those hours, just strumming early versions of 'Best Friend' and songs that have now been incorporated into other songs, so bloody loudly he couldn't hear me screaming like a virago at him to hurry up. This apparent sacrilege might have prevented a few masterpieces from coming to fruition, but really you try wheeling barrows of concrete all day and find yourself unable to get into the bathroom because there's some lunatic in there who says the acoustics are good! Anyway, I did suggest that perhaps he and Andy (who also played guitar) ought to get a band together and practice somewhere other than the bathroom. [xi]

In fact, quite a few of the songs that later featured on *Special Beat Service* were originally written by Wakeling in a room with a window overlooking the ocean. According to Wakeling:

It was absolutely beautiful. You could see the ocean on the horizon, which I wasn't used to in Birmingham. [xii]

When they weren't busy working, Wakeling and Cox played their guitars and wrote songs that would later be recorded for all three of their future albums. But they quickly realized that if they wanted to start a band they needed a rhythm section, so they advertised for a bass player in the local Isle of Wight newspaper. They received only one response from a local 17-year-old punk bassist named David Steele. Cox recalled the initial meeting:

This fellow called up and said, 'I play bass. What kind of music do you like?' Andy, who'd been buying loads of punk

*singles from the record shop in town, reeled off names – the
Clash, Culture, Siouxsie and the Banshees... but the
Buzzcocks and U Roy were the groups that clinched it.
David Steele made arrangements to meet the Brummies in
town that Saturday.* [xiii]

Hebrides recalled the first meeting between Steele, Wakeling, and
Cox:

*David had answered an advertisement in the local I.O.W.
newspaper for a bass guitarist to 'shake some action!' David
(at the time a punk with a taste for lurid clothing) said
afterwards that his first impression of Andy was he looked
like a 'northern weirdo' and that Dave looked like 'some kind
of grapefruit salesman.' He was probably right.* [xiv]

If there was some initial social awkwardness, the trio connected
musically and agreed on a diverse musical approach. Wakeling
noted this in Daniel Rachel's oral history, *Walls Come Tumbling
Down*:

*My first notion of the Beat was the industrial angst of the
Velvet Underground with the joie de vivre and the survival
message of Toots and the Maytals, and Petula Clarke, and
the Buzzcocks on top; and then I got be to Bryan Ferry and
Van Morrison and Tim Buckley, if I could get the notes.* [xv]

As it turned out, Steele had been accepted into a mental health nurse training program at All Saints Hospital in Birmingham allowing him to keep playing with Wakeling and Cox. This was serendipitous, as both had decided they'd had enough of the Isle of Wight and were ready to head home. Upon their return to Birmingham, the trio, in search of a drummer, were introduced to Everett Morton through a nursing colleague Steele met at the hospital.

Morton wasn't a drummer when he left St. Kitts to immigrate to England in the mid-60s. He found work in a tea kettle factory in Birmingham where he beat out rhythms on hollow sheets of metal when he was bored. He soon realized he had talent, and after a stint at a drum school and constant practice on his furniture at home, developed his own unique, polyrhythmic style. He soon began playing in bands around the Handsworth section of Birmingham, where many Caribbean immigrants had settled.

The first time Morton met Wakeling, Steele, and Cox and listened to them bash out their proto punk songs on acoustic guitars he was perplexed but also intrigued:

> *Couldn't make nothing of it, the music was so strange; that was why I wanted to work with them, because it was so different.* [xvi]

It was rough going at first. Morton was a reggae drummer, but the other three didn't have experience playing the genre. While they listened to reggae frequently, they had been playing in a punk style. Wakeling noted in an interview with *The Face*, that Morton was wary of anything to do with punk and that he was a better musician than the rest of them:

> *Everett was pretty frightened of anything you could call punk, I think, so he put it all in straight 4's on the bass drum and that's what gives it the drum machine sound. He's such a strong player and he was so much better than the rest of us when we began that if he thought we were going wrong he'd just stop us dead with a roll – we'd stand there open-mouthed until he let us back in.* [xvii]

The band secured a Tuesday night residency at the Mercat Cross in Birmingham, a "meat market" pub, which was one of the few that did not enforce a "No Punks, No Rastas" policy. It was there that they met a charismatic 16-year-old named Roger Charlery – the son of immigrants from St Lucia -- who had dubbed himself Ranking Roger.   Roger, a reggae-loving punk, was often at the pub and would hop up on stage to toast and dance during the foursome's reggae numbers. According to an *NME* interview from 1980, Wakeling recalled how Roger joined the band:

Roger used to stage-crash: jump on the mic and toast to a song with the band, invited or not. He turned up at a gig in Moseley and did one number. Then he came to the next gig and did the same, and then he did two numbers at one gig and it became slowly obvious that he had to join the band full time. [xviii]

When interviewed by the *NME* in early 1980, Roger shared that his initial approach for those early shows was completely improvisational:

A lot of the time I just say the first thing that comes into my head. 'Ranking Full Stop' was like that. If you listen to the single and the version on our John Peel session, they are completely different. It was only about three weeks ago that I learnt the words all by heart for the first time. As for 'Tears Of A Clown,' I still don't know the first verse. [xix]

As word got out about the band, their shows became more crowded, and Roger started joining the band on stage for their entire set. After the residency at the Mercat Cross ended, the band asked Roger to join as a full-time member. Amazingly, he'd also been offered a chance to be in UB40, having joined them on stage as their first toaster/MC in their early days, but preferred the Beat's punkier vibe.

During the summer and fall of 1979, the now five-piece band with Roger in tow began playing more shows, including a support slot for the Selecter. It was at this first show that Neol Davies, guitarist of the Selecter, listened to the band's soundcheck and offered them the opportunity to open any shows they wanted in return for gas money.

According to Steele, this series of shows with the Selecter – who had benefitted from having their instrumental track "The Selecter" featured on the B-side of the Specials first 2 Tone single release -- changed the band's trajectory:

> *These gigs were so fast and so amazing: the whole buzz and excitement. We'd been playing in little pubs to about twenty people and then it was fifty, then a hundred and now it was five hundred and another five hundred outside.* xx

The final piece of the puzzle was the addition of the spiritual guru of the group, Augustus "Saxa" Martin, a Jamaican immigrant who joined after auditioning for the band. Morton was the connection to Saxa; they frequented the same pub in Handsworth and played gigs together. Saxa was a well-known character around Birmingham with a musical legacy that included backing '60s ska and reggae artists Desmond Dekker, Laurel Aitken, and Prince Buster when they toured England. Roger remembered meeting Saxa for the first time and being intimidated by him, but then quickly warmed to a man old enough to be his grandfather:

> *When he came along, he was loud, he was shouting, and he was drinking. But as soon as he blew that horn... he proved that you should never judge a book by its cover. At first, it was like he was saying 'This band is my band'. In the end, we were his band! He wasn't wrong and his presence meant we were three generations in one band.* xxi

Hebrides met Saxa for the first time with Morton and Cox at a local Birmingham pub:

> *I went with Everett and Andy one night to the New Inns in Handsworth to see the man Everett was suggesting as a possible saxophone player to do a few sessions with the band. A jazz band was playing in the corner and the sax player was amazing – I'd never seen one so good just playing in a pub. Later he came along to the Mercat Cross (where the Beat had a residency from June to September 1979) to jam with them and after the gig he kept laughing and saying, 'you're my boys y'know – I like you boys, you're my boys.' They liked him too, and so Saxa's been with them ever since. He never practiced with them before those early gigs –*

he's a jazz musician who can improvise to anything from
Dizzy Gillespie to Irish ballads. It was perfect every time. xxii

With Saxa now in the fold, this odd collection of bandmates across
three generations seemed drawn to one another as if by a strange
centrifugal force. As Wakeling explained:

It was a magical confluence of people. It was the first person
we met who played that instrument that came into the
group and it ended up with an age difference [of] 16 to 59.
Because of that, we didn't always see eye to eye, but that
wasn't important, really. It was more important that we
could pull the best ideas out of the six of us and the best
ones ended up in the song and that created a kind of magic
that we couldn't have consciously made if we had tried. xxiii

During this time the band began playing more shows in London,
and after one of their biggest shows at the Electric Ballroom with
the Selecter, they were approached backstage by Jerry Dammers:
founder of 2 Tone Records and a member of the Specials. He offered
them a one-off deal to record a single for the label. Roger noted how
the deal with 2 Tone came about:

We had sent a demo to Jerry Dammers and he came with
Lynval Golding to one of the dates the Beat gigged with the

Selecter and they were dancing down in front with Neol and Pauline. Then the last gig of the tour at the Electric Ballroom, Jerry came again with his briefcase and he had some papers: 'We really like you guys and want you to be the next 2 Tone band. Can you do a single within three days? We were like, WHAT! [xxiv]

Shortly after meeting Saxa, the band opened a show in early October 1979 for the legendary BBC Radio One broadcaster John Peel at Aston University in Birmingham. After playing their set, Peel described them as "*the best band in the world apart from the Undertones.*" After the gig, the band invited Peel out for dinner at the Ladypool Road curry house to thank him for his support. According to Wakeling:

We were sitting there with John, just so full of ourselves, and a car came around the corner and smashed into our blue van. That put a dampener on things, but he said, 'I'd better give you a Peel Session to pay for that.' [xxv]

Peel Sessions were a defining feature of BBC Radio One from 1967 to 2004. Born out of restrictions imposed on the BBC, these sessions allowed bands to record four tracks at the broadcaster's Maida Vale studios. Somewhere between a live performance and a demo, these sessions were often recorded in a single day. Over the years, roughly 4,000 sessions were recorded by over 2,000 artists.

The band's first Peel session was recorded on October 24, 1979, just a few weeks after they had met the legendary DJ, and their session was first broadcast on the BBC on November 5, 1979. It featured early, nascent versions of "Tears Of A Clown," "Mirror In The Bathroom," "Ranking Full Stop," "Click Click," and "Big Shot." Notably, the songs don't include Saxa who hadn't officially joined yet. Wakeling noted that the Peel session captured the raw energy of a band still finding its way:

> *You can hear that earnestness on it, but we really didn't know what we were doing. We were having to walk with our shoulders back and pretend we did. You can feel that youthful nervousness trying to come across as swagger, and I find the combination of the two to be really charming. I hadn't heard the John Peel sessions for years, and the songs were recorded before we got a record deal – before we even KNEW we had a record deal, and certainly before we had any dreams of becoming a successful group, being in the charts, any of that. It was quite pure. Not so far to say innocent, but certainly naïve. There's a certain charm to them, so I listen to them and it definitely brings me back to*

that enthusiasm and that 'we can change the world' sort of
feeling. xxvi

The session was produced by Peel's in-house producer Bob
Sargeant, who was immediately impressed with the band:

> *They were very nervous, it being their first session. I tried to*
> *put them at ease. When they started to play it was*
> *immediately very fresh and exciting. I particularly thought*
> *Dave Wakeling had a great voice. We were trying to get it*
> *live and immediate, and as a result the session went very*
> *quick, and we had five numbers done by 7:30pm. Then the*
> *manager rolled in. He said the band had had a chat in the*
> *canteen, they were recording a single for 2 Tone in a few*
> *days, and would I like to produce it? I think they were*
> *simply pleased at having a very well-engineered session.* xxvii

Sargeant entered the music business in the '60s, joining UK
regional R&B act Junco Partners as a keyboardist, and the group
released a lone album and a few singles in the early '70s. Their
claim to fame was opening for Led Zeppelin's first gig. While
success eluded him as a musician, Sargeant made his mark behind
the sound board. During Sargeant's time at the BBC, he recorded
Peel Sessions for Joy Division, the Cure, Gary Numan, Killing

Joke, Motorhead, Stiff Little Fingers, Gang of Four, Wire, Dexy's Midnight Runners, and many more.

Simultaneously, Sargeant began working as an independent producer, starting with the Fall's 1978 debut, *Live at the Witch Trials* (a personal favorite of Steele's), followed by the Ruts' *The Crack* in 1979 and the Monochrome Set's *Strange Boutique* in 1980. He later became a hot commodity for his production work with the Beat.

In addition to tapping Sargeant to produce, the band asked Saxa if he would be interested in joining them on the 2 Tone recording of "Tears Of A Clown." According to Wakeling:

> *...so we said to him one Thursday night, "Do you do records?" He said, "Yeah, sure." "Would you like to do one Saturday, then?" "Yes." So he played on "Tears of a Clown.*
>
> *I think we did one show first, and I had him stand next to me. I wasn't much of a musician myself, certainly not theoretically. For me, what key the song was, was whatever my first chord was on the guitar. Which is not true, but that's what it was to me. So each song would start, and when I got the chance, I'd look at him and say, 'It's in G,' or: 'It's in C.' Sometimes I was right, and sometimes I wasn't.*

49

Halfway through the set he said, 'Don't worry, David, me know all the keys. Me know them all!'

He would just go off and change the timing and play the melody backwards. We'd all be looking at each other terrified. We wouldn't really know if we were on the end of the second beat or what. Everybody's looking at me like, 'Well, you should know where to come in singing. It's your song.' We were completely lost. We'd just have to wait 'til Saxa stopped, and the crowd would clap, then we'd go, '1, 2, 3, 4... Ok, here we are...' [xxviii]

Originally Chrysalis, who distributed 2-Tone singles, wanted the band to release "Mirror in the Bathroom," but the initial offer on the table was that Chrysalis would own the song. This didn't sit well with the band. According to Wakeling:

So, Jerry Dammers came to us, told us about 2-Tone, and came and saw the band. He said, 'Would you like to do a single for 2-Tone,' and we said 'Yes, we'd love to, thanks.' And he said, 'We really liked that 'Mirror In The Bathroom' song.' And we said, 'That's probably our best song. Yeah, that would be a good one.' Then he came back a week or so later and he said, 'Oh, Chrysalis says you can do 'Mirror In The Bathroom,' they like it, but they would own the rights to it for five years.' We're like, 'No.' I said, 'You know, that's our best tune. We'd want it on our album. But so long as we can bring it out on our album, that would be fine, you can have it as a single.' So he went off again and he came back, and he said, 'No, Chrysalis said if it's the single it can't be on your first album.'

So we said, 'Well, tell them to fuck themselves.' and we said, 'We'll do 'Tears Of A Clown' then.' Because that always goes down great. And you can tell the fellows at Chrysalis they can argue with Stevie Wonder and Smokey Robinson about whose song it is. And so we just insisted, and as luck would have it, our song came out in October and by December 6 it was #6 in the charts, and it was the runaway dance party hit of the Christmas of '79. It was on every jukebox and every turntable for every Christmas party. So I think it probably worked out really well, because I don't know if 'Mirror In The Bathroom' would have been that cheery as a Christmas single. [xxix]

The Beat were the hottest unsigned band in Britain in late 1979 and the success of the 2 Tone release of "Tears Of A Clown" set off a fierce record company bidding war. A tape of the first Peel session was passed along to Simon Potts, who worked in A&R for Arista Records.

Potts began his professional career as a salesman for ABC Records and quickly advanced into becoming a promotion man after escorting BB King on radio interviews around London. On the side, Potts also promoted Joy Division and the Ruts before joining Arista Records, eventually rising to become the head of the A&R department. He later worked with everyone from the Thompson Twins and Patti Smith to the Cure, Aretha Franklin, Radiohead, and the Butthole Surfers.

But, before all that, the Beat were his very first signing. According to Potts:

> *I'd seen a band around London called the Specials. I told my managing director [at Arista Records] about it, a guy called Charles Levison, and said 'We should sign this group.' He said, 'Oh get back in your corner, son. You don't know what you're talking about.' As it happened, that record went to number one, it was called 'Gangsters.'*

> *A month or so after that happened, Charles asked me if I wanted to move into A&R. Very excitedly, I went to Radio*

*One and ran into John Peel. He said, 'I saw a band the other
night called the Beat.' So I went up to see the band, I
thought they were great, and the audience was fantastic -
they really responded to them - and eventually I worked my
way backstage.*

*I met the manager Mick Hancock, met the band and talked
to them about life in general, that I worked for Arista
Records, and that I'd like to sign them to the record label. I
didn't know what that entailed at the time...*

*But I knew that persistence would pay off. I was at every gig
from there on in. I find out wherever they would play around
the north of England and I'd be there. I was the persistent
one. There were other A&R men who came and went, we
had competition.*

*'Mirror In The Bathroom' was the song that, when I saw
them live, I thought would be the crossover, if there was to
be such a thing. The crossover single. That's the song that
has stood the test of time.* xxx

Arista had competition from 2 Tone and other labels in the UK, but
Potts was motivated and creative, offering the band an
extraordinary deal with Arista: their own boutique label called Go

Feet records. Because the band liked and trusted Potts and were impressed with the offer of their own label, they had him insured for a hefty sum of money, so, in the event of his death, they could pay off their debt to Arista and be free to sign elsewhere if Potts' replacement was not someone they cared to deal with. According to Roger, that specific detail was what convinced the band to sign with the label:

> *We went for Arista, who were offering us less money but the most freedom we wanted. So it wasn't about money for the Beat, it was about having your own say within that crooked business and people who'd actually listen to you. Because someone could offer you a million pounds and just put you on the shelf. But the guys at Arista said: Listen, whatever we do, whoever you sign with, it doesn't matter. But if you sign with us, we're gonna break this band and make sure this band gets the recognition, and they did.* [xxxi]

With support from Arista and all the excitement generated by their connection to 2 Tone, *I Just Can't Stop It* quickly rose up the UK pop charts lifted by a trio of singles: "Tears Of A Clown," "Hands Off... She's Mine," and then "Mirror In The Bathroom." The records peaked at #6, #14, and #4 respectively. By the end of 1980 the album appeared on numerous lists of best albums of the year: *NME* ranked it 3rd, *Sounds* ranked it 13th and *The Village Voice* ranked it 21st.

Interestingly, Morton, ever the gentleman and consummate reggae drummer by nature, still felt the songs from the first record were too fast. During an interview with the band's fan club newsletter "Noise In This World" after *I Just Can't Stop It* was released he said:

> *...in interviews I didn't like to say anything but I didn't think it was reggae. I'd call it reggae destroyed by punk; much too fast for me. You could bop to the songs, but dancing? Not what I'd call dancing, but these days I suppose a lot of different movements count as dancing.*[xxxii]

Hot on the heels on the success of the chart success of *I Just Can't Stop It* and the European and U.S. tours to promote it, Arista informed the band that they needed to record a follow-up immediately. According to Cox:

> *It's great when somebody asks you to make that first album. You've got the songs and you've played them for a couple of years. You've been thinking about the whole thing for five years... so you just go in and do it all on nervous energy. Then you spend the next seven months touring and*

> *promoting – trying to sell the thing. And then one day*
> *someone from the record company finds you and says, 'Oh*
> *boy, you know you should've delivered us another album*
> *yesterday.' So you say, 'Hang on. We've been on the road and*
> *we haven't any songs – we've been trying to survive in all*
> *these countries.'* *xxxiii*

According to Cox, the band wrote *Wha'ppen* in about three weeks
and recorded it in 6 weeks:

> *…because it was time for a new album. We just wrote it and*
> *went straight in and recorded it, so it's a bit like a jigsaw*
> *puzzle.* *xxxiv*

Instead of the amped up, punky reggae of their debut, *Wha'ppen*
delved into a wide variety of additional 'riddims' including dub,
calypso, and various hybrids of their own creation. Likewise, the
lyrics explored the complications and disappointment that occur
when personal relations intersect with political concerns. Reviews
in the UK were mixed; some in the music media were quick to pan
the album, claiming the Beat had lost their way. Others, like the
Record Mirror, were much more generous in their take:

> *What's consistent about the Beat is their charm, their*
> *ability to capture and express a sense of drowning, or letting*

go, of surrendering to delight, while keeping their finger on the unpleasant pleasures of contemporary Britain. Who else would put together as neurotic a lyric as "Drowning" with as tempting a melody? xxxv

Here in the US, *Trouser Press* give the release a full-throated, full-page review, stating unequivocally:

Wha'ppen presents a band that, far from suffocating in a dated trend, has shed its Two-Tone chrysalis for full-fledged individuality. It's a breathtakingly vital record.[xxxvi]

But the review also cautioned that success in America could take time or not ever happen:

If the US shrugged off I Just Can't Stop It's non-stop dance party, how will it take this comparatively laid-back offering? There's almost no way mass cult America can deal with this album. Radio will ignore it, record stores will bury it. That leaves a pitiably small coterie to spread the word.[xxxvii]

Despite a slower sound and slower sales, *Wha'ppen* peaked at number 3 on the UK albums chart and featured on many best of lists at the end of 1981. It also served as a jumping off point for the songs that would go on to make-up *Special Beat Service*.

Now with two albums under their belts, an amazing live show and growing critical acclaim, the band are poised to release their third album *Special Beat Service* on I.R.S. Records in America. And so, on this early fall Saturday morning in Hollywood they are ready to be beamed into the homes of the American teenage record buying public.

I.R.S. Records – founded by Miles Copeland and Jay Boberg in 1979, was perhaps the single most important record label of the post-punk/new wave era. Copeland was already an important figure in the UK's punk and new wave scene, dabbling in artist management, show promotion, as well as a bit of music and magazine production.

At the time, Copeland was managing his brother Stewart's band, a new trio called the Police. A year earlier they had released their debut album which contained the hit single "Roxanne" (UK #12, U.S. #32). At the time, Boberg was working for A&M Records as a college representative and one of the bands he was promoting was the Police.

Though based primarily in London, Copeland approached Jerry Moss at A&M Records in Los Angeles about forming a subsidiary label of sorts that would become the International Record Syndicate or I.R.S. Records. A&M, who had the Police on their roster, had been founded in 1962 by jazz musician and bandleader Herb Alpert and record executive Moss. No strangers to promoting music outside of the pop mainstream, they agreed to distribute the new label with Copeland and Boberg maintaining ownership. Copeland told Cash Box in March 1980:

> *I had established a good track record with A&M England. I brought them Squeeze at a time when they needed a young act, having just been burned by the Sex Pistols and the Stranglers, who went out of their way to offend everybody. We toured and made a good impression on everyone. Then I brought them the Police, toured them without a record, and showed them you could break an act without spending a fortune. So finally, when I came to Jerry Moss with the I.R.S. concept, I made it clear it was an opportunity he couldn't afford to pass on.*[xxxviii]

Interestingly, there was an early connection between the Police and the English Beat, who toured together frequently in the early 80s. For many young American viewers the sight of Sting wearing a Beat girl t-shirt in the 1981 music documentary *Urgh! A Music War* and in the MTV video for the band's wildly popular "Don't Stand So Close To Me" was great branding for the band. The t-shirt took on enormous cachet among early 80s teens in the know. According to

Wakeling – who called the Police "The Monkees of punk" there was a coded message in Sting's decision to wear the t-shirt:

> *Touring with the Police was an odd situation — they were ruled by fear by Miles Copeland. They were not allowed to speak their minds. They were heavily contained, and we felt very sad for them, really, because they did have ideas and opinions that they were banned from being able to say. I think that was one of the reasons that he (Sting) went to such extremes to wear English Beat T-shirts, like in the "Don't Stand So Close To Me" video and photo sessions: He was trying to, like, bear allegiance to some of the things we were saying that he was not allowed to say by Miles Copeland.* [xxxix]

The first release on I.R.S. was a collection of singles by punk band the Buzzcocks. The label then had some early chart success, particularly in the UK, where several of its artists posted top-40 singles. However, it was an all-girl group from Los Angeles that would land the label near the top of the charts in the US. In 1981, the Go-Go's released *Beauty and the Beat* on I.R.S. The album featured the hits "Our Lips Are Sealed (U.S. #20) (co-written by band guitarist Jane Wiedlin and Terry Hall of the Specials and Fun Boy Three) and "We Got the Beat" (U.S. #2). It was at this point in time, that the label, who had also signed Berlin, the Dead

Kennedys, and Oingo Boingo on the label, set their sights on signing the English Beat.

I.R.S. wooed the English Beat away from Sire in the US in August 1982 and their first appearance on *American Bandstand* was part of an ambitious plan to break the band in America. As it turns out, the band were excited about the opportunity with I.R.S. after several frustrating years at Sire, which by 1982 was in the process of being swallowed up by Warner Brothers.

The band's first two releases on Sire Records in the US sold upward of 100,000 units each which made I.R.S. optimistic about their chances for success with their third album. Steele shared the band's perspective on the switch from Sire to I.R.S. during a college radio interview he did on KTRU-FM in 1982:

> *Sire don't really understand us. It's really weird because people think Sire are great. They've got all these good groups like Depeche Mode and Talking Heads. It's like a big con really. I.R.S. seem really keen and compared to most American record companies they're really good. They are quite human. You can even say the odd sentence to them,*

and they understand. Most big American record companies
are in a totally different universe.[xl]

The I.R.S. brass hoped that the release of *Special Beat Service* in
October 1982 would solidify them as a "new wave" band and that
this new sound – which was a hard turn from the sound of their two
previous LPs would broaden their appeal. According to a *Billboard*
story that November, initial sales of *Special Beat Service* in the
U.S. were encouraging with the label selling 50,000 copies between
its release date of October 1st and mid-November 1982.[xli]

Unlike most major labels of the time, I.R.S. was unwilling and
unable to afford the payola game then in vogue with top 40
American radio programmers. Payola was the undercover or
indirect payment of money to deejays or radio stations to play a
song without disclosing the payment. Instead, the label looked for
creative ways to reach a new audience, hence *American Bandstand*
– which despite lower ratings in the early 80s still set the tone and
pace for teenage style and attitudes and leaned heavily on band's
then popular on college radio.

Boberg's independent, do-it-yourself approach at I.R.S. was unique
for the music business of the time and critical to the work that went
into breaking the band in the US. According to a profile in the

August 14, 1982 edition of *Billboard*, the I.R.S marketing method
was best described as "...the importance of common sense":

> *Boberg proposed "alternative marketing" for exposing new*
> *bands, as a way of getting around the ever-tightening radio*
> *market. Describing his "building-block theory," Boberg*
> *offered touring as "the most effective way of spreading the*
> *word—breaking your band from the street," pointing out the*
> *mid-west's ideal location for developing a strong regional*
> *base. He advised utilizing local press, retail, college radio*
> *and dance clubs at all stops on the itinerary. Boberg*
> *suggested a paraphernalia blitz as further means of creating*
> *buzz: T-shirts, buttons, stickers ("they're great – they're very*
> *difficult to get off things") and the all-important record.*[xlii]

I.R.S. went all in on servicing college radio and began offering an
affordable $25 annual subscription service to college stations. All
new I.R.S. releases, promotional materials, artist itineraries and
back catalog were made available to subscribers ensuring airplay.
I.R.S. also coordinated promotion of their artist's touring schedules
with local college radio stations, smartly understanding that people
who attended concerts might have only learned about the artist
because they heard about them on the radio. In their estimation
this targeted promotion should increase audience size and record
sales. According to Wakeling:

Miles [Copeland] had collected some very interesting people around him. Certainly, there was a point of stasis in the music business surrounding radio; it seemed to cost so much money to get a top 40 station to play your song that only the wealthy and entrenched could even play the game. And so, I thought it was a clever idea for I.R.S. to try and circumvent that by not paying any attention at all, instead applying all their talent, time, energy, and what money they had to things like college radio, which was cheaper but also could get you a lot of direct contact with your niche audience.[xliii]

While I watched the band live for the first time that day on my small black and white TV, they were a blur of kinetic energy and movement performing "Save It For Later," and "Sugar and Stress." I was not familiar with either song, and the whole performance went by so quickly that I didn't have time to really register it all. But I was joyful in a way I hadn't been for a long time.

Seeing 19-year-old Roger hop, skip and jump back and forth across the small TV studio sound stage was mesmerizing. Though only two years older than me, he was living the life of rock and pop stardom that enthralled me. Dressed in his signature black hat, white shirt with black tie and black pants, he looked every bit the 2 Tone rude boy I desperately aspired to be. The loud cat calls from the largely female audience in the ABC Television Center studio suggested that Wakeling and Roger were scream-worthy pop stars in the making. And based on his friendly banter with the band, Clark appeared to be a fan too. Wakeling later confirmed this:

> *Dick Clark was amazing; his wife put info cards about every band member on his desk the day of each show, which he memorized. When he came into our dressing room, he knew our names, asked kind and relevant questions, and our hearts just melted.*[xliv]

During the interview, I was struck by Wakeling's Midlands accent. It's the first time I'd ever heard him speak. I'd never met anyone from England before and he spoke in a melodic sing-song lilt as he explained why the band were called the English Beat in America: an American version of the Beat led by Paul Collins got to the name first. Wakeling later explained the other name options the band had considered at Arista's urging:

> *The English Beat was a better choice than Beat UK, or British Beat, which the record label wanted. We first picked Beat Bros, but the label said it sounded like an R'n'B act. One morning we saw English muffins on a New York breakfast menu, and guessed Americans thought the word English was cute.* [xlv]

Clark asked Roger – who I now desperately want to be friends with, to introduce the rest of his bandmates, who remain mute. I immediately noticed that Saxa was missing. Clark also had the same question, and Wakeling ended up using the rest of the interview to explain how Saxa joined the band and now, several years into a grueling tour schedule, has officially retired from the road. In his place he points at saxophone session man extraordinaire Wesley Magoogan standing to his left. I file that tidbit of new, personal band information away in my brain. It has been a good morning alone in my room and I play *I Just Can't Stop It* and *Wha'ppen* in quick succession.

The timing of the band's signing to I.R.S. in 1982 coincided with one of the biggest outdoor music festivals in history. Apple co-founder Steve Wozniak hatched an ambitious and very expensive musical plan and committed a large chunk of his sizeable fortune to a musical event, billed as the biggest thing since Woodstock. Wozniak staged a three-day concert in the mountains of San Bernardino County, in Southern California, that featured some of the day's biggest names in music. The "US Festival" kicked off under scorching conditions on September 3, 1982.

Wozniak, then 32 years old and on leave from Apple after a plane crash left him unable to form memories for half a year, spent 18 months and $13 million of his own money preparing what he dubbed "the Super Bowl of rock." He intended it as a unifying antidote to the just-ended "Me Decade" - a benevolent we-are-the-world event evident beamed by satellite – during the height of the cold war to the Soviet Union.

Sparing no expense, Wozniak aimed to bring together many of the top artists of the day, segregated by genre: new wave, heavy metal, and traditional rock, enhanced by cutting-edge innovation, including the first use of jumbo video screens at a concert. According to Wakeling, Wozniak seemed to have good intentions:

> *He seemed really affable and oddly humble – not like your normal multimillionaire. The question of why you would want a quarter of a million people in the field in 120-degree weather just to celebrate is another question that's not for me to ponder. But he seemed to have his heart in it.*[xlvi]

Produced by Bay Area music legend Bill Graham, the talent amassed for the first festival played out like several stadium concerts crammed together. Despite sluggish pre-sales, the festival drew 425,000 concert goers across the weekend. Prices for the festival: $17 per day, $35 for the weekend.

The opening day of US '82 featured a staggeringly strong lineup of the best new wave bands of the early 80s: Gang of Four, the Ramones, the English Beat, Oingo Boingo, the B-52's, Talking Heads and the Police who performed before more than 100,000 fans. An *LA Magazine* retrospective from 2017 set the scene:

> *Moments after Gang of Four kicked off the weekend on a scorching Friday afternoon, it was apparent this was not your hippie dad's rock festival. Powered by 400,000 watts, the audio was crisp and clear, and attendees could see the stage from anywhere, thanks to strategically placed video screens—an innovative concept that offered pristine viewing even during the daytime.* [xlvii]

The size of the crowd was a shock for the band which had primarily been playing 10,000 capacity concert halls. As Roger remembers:

> *When I walked out at the US Festival, I was confronted with a sea of faces as far as the eye could see. I was like, "My God! Where do you start here?" We were so nervous. That was the biggest gig we ever did. It was the biggest gig any musician had ever done. Playing in front of half a million people. It was like, "How are they going to hear us in time at the back?* [xlviii]

Five songs into their US Festival set, Roger unveiled the new breezy pop direction of *Special Beat Service* when he shouted into his mic: "*We got a new album coming out soon. It's going to be our third album and it's going to be called Special Beat Service. So, listen up for it. Here's a track off it called "I Confess."* Right on cue, classically trained keyboardist and former skinhead Dave "Blockhead" Wright began to play a Latin piano melody reminiscent of tracks off Joe Jackson's recent American smash *Night and Day*.

Wright, who originally joined the band to handle sound and lighting and then did a short stint as their tour manager, had lived in St. Kitts in the eastern Caribbean in the mid 60s where he joined a calypso band called the Casanovas. It was that experience that informed his melodic playing on all the new songs the band debuted that afternoon. According to Wright, the genesis for the catchy piano on "I Confess" came from the rhythm for the 1974 U.S. pop smash "Rock The Boat" by the Hues Corporation.

> *I just loved the rhythm of that, right? And I used to mess around with it. And on one occasion, Dave Wakeling walked by and sat by me, and we had a little chat and then the next day, he came back, and he's got these lyrics that he'd started to wrap around the lick. And all I remember is that it*

seemed to happen very, very quickly with a minimal amount of effort. [xlix]

It is cerebral and sophisticated pop of the highest order and Cox's skanking guitar has been replaced with soulful strumming that augments Magoogan's melodic and angular saxophone runs. While all this is happening behind them, Wakeling and Roger are harmonizing like a new wave Everly Brothers. The band sound is so tight that its hard to tell where Wakeling's voice begins and Roger's ends. Wright remembered the experience for the dust clouds kicked up by all the people dancing:

> *And as we were playing, they started to get into it quite quickly. And then by about halfway through the set, suddenly this cloud of dust appeared. You couldn't see the back of it. It was just dust everywhere. And that slowly drifted towards the stage. So the stage got covered in dust. This is just coming from people dancing. We had a few more gigs. I remember I had trouble with the keyboards for every single gig after that, because this fine sand that had got in.*

> *I think the great memory of that was that to see an audience starting off interested, enjoying it and see them start moving the feet a bit, and dancing a bit. And then quite a lot*

of them are going quite wild by the end, which is just a great feeling.¹

Near the end of the set, the band performed "Save It For Later" from *Special Beat Service*. In the audience that day was 17-year-old Ed Severson, who was there to see the Talking Heads. Severson, who later changed his last name to his mother's maiden name – Vedder was moved by "Save It For Later":

> *Right around this time – still a teenager himself – Ed writes a song with a similar vocal melody, chord progression, and theme. It is also, in a way, about promise and disappointment – about being lost, and trying to find your place in the world – and will be recorded twelve years later: "Better Man"* [li]

Despite the rapturous reaction from the 1982 US festival crowd, selling *Special Beat Service* to an American audience will be an uphill slog. Wright remembered the US Festival performance being a key turning point for the band:

> *I think there'd been a feeling around that as far as back home in the UK was concerned, the whole 2 Tone thing was dead and buried. It wasn't quite, but that's what we all felt about it. But things were going well in America. So I think*

71

that feeling of certain things having come to an end in the UK had an impact overall, even if things were going well in America. I think it caused fissures to develop. But it wasn't just that, it was other things. I think there were certain disagreements about what we do and how we do it. We toured, and toured, and toured, and toured. And to be honest, I was perfectly happy with that. But not everybody was very happy with that. A couple of people were very tired and exhausted, not only tired exhausted, but thought "we can do better than this. We can do different than this."[lii]

One week before Christmas 1982, *Special Beat Service* debuted on the Billboard Rock Albums chart at number 48. By mid-February 1983 it had inched up to number 38.

Special Beat Service immediately appealed to the outsider in me that had been germinating since I was young. I'd always been a sensitive kid and until a recent growth spurt, small for my age. I had a full head of very curly hair – to be honest it was a Jewfro -- that my mother loved but I hated. It drew attention and I was often teased for it and called "tumbleweed" or "bush." And, despite my desire to just go with the flow of life, I felt things deeply. While most kids my age seemed carefree, I worried a lot and preferred my own company and was more comfortable speaking to adults. They seemed to get where I was coming from. The way I saw it, kids my own age were mean, and the meanest ones seemed to relish taking advantage of my easygoing nature and extreme gullibility. I was an easy mark.

This sense of not quite fitting in was exacerbated by two moves in the span of three years. I was eight years old in 1973 when we moved from Princeton, New Jersey to Medfield, Massachusetts. When I was eleven, we moved again, this time from Medfield back to Princeton. Instead of giving me a tougher skin, the moves made me feel more vulnerable and alone.

The first move in 1973, which came at the height of the Watergate scandal and the last days of the Vietnam War, was particularly hard on me. As the expanding political crisis engulfed the country there was a growing crisis looming in my own home. My parents' marriage was beginning to show very significant signs of unraveling.

On top of that, my six-year-old sister Wendy and I were the only Jewish kids at our local elementary school. Though I didn't experience any overt anti-Semitism (that would come much later, in high school), I didn't quite fit in at a school that was nearly 100% Irish and Italian Catholic. Then, in early 1974, Wendy was diagnosed with a severe case of ulcerative colitis. She spent a lot of time in and out of Boston Children's Hospital, and I spent a lot of time in the waiting room with my distressed parents.

At nine, I was beginning to search for ways to make sense of a life that felt disconnected. My parents were distracted by my sister's illness and by their own marital drama. But I discovered that music spoke to me. Car rides became time for me to disappear into music playing on the radio, and I asked my parents incessant questions about who was singing each song, what the song was about, and why these 3 minutes and 30 seconds of pop music were giving me butterflies in my stomach.

At some point my mother decided to take me to the local Lords department store in downtown Medfield. A small section of the store stocked 45 singles popular on the Billboard charts. Slowly, I began to put together the link between what I was hearing on the radio and the vinyl versions I could buy and take home to listen to whenever I wanted. Once I had my own records, I listened carefully and began to take note of lyrics that moved me.

These singles become a refuge and featured stories of injustice, sacrifice, and the emotional pain endured by the characters in each song. I imagined the backstory of the protagonist in "Billy Don't Be A Hero" by Bo Donaldson & The Heywoods, and I worried about him, particularly as the war in Viet Nam was coming to an end:

> *...The soldier blues were trapped on a hillside/The battle ragin' all around/The sergeant cried 'We've gotta' hang on, boys/We gotta' hold this piece of ground...*

I was a wreck when I learned that Billy dies in the end. Helen Reddy's version of "Delta Dawn" also haunted me. Despite the upbeat, gospel-tinged choir, Delta Dawn goes insane searching in vain for her lost love:

> *...She's forty-one and her daddy still calls her 'baby'/All the folks around Brownsville say she's crazy/'Cause she walks downtown with a suitcase in her hand/Looking for a mysterious dark-haired man...*

And Cher's "Half Breed" painted a vibrant picture of racism rarely heard on pop radio:

> *...Half breed that's all I ever heard/Half breed how I learned to hate the word/Half breed she's no good they warned/Both sides were against me since the day I was born...*

It broke my young heart. Terry Jack's 1974 hit "Seasons in The Sun" about a dying man made me worry even more about my sister.

...Goodbye my friend, it's hard to die/When all the birds are singing in the sky...

Much to my relief, my parents announced we were moving back to Princeton in the summer of 1976. But my relief was short lived. My father lost several jobs in quick succession and as part of his frustration and angst began to distance himself from us each night after dinner by falling asleep in front of the TV in our family room.

In contrast, my mother had started down a path of late 70's self-discovery that included several weekend stints at EST seminars, followed by weekly appointments with a local psychologist who urged her to go to Al-Anon meetings to deal with the impact of her father's alcoholism. I coped by burrowing deeper into music, listening more and more to the radio, and using my small allowance to buy more singles and albums.

I became a devotee of WKTU-FM which had changed to an all-disco format and was now the number one radio station in New York due in part to the faddish popularity of songs featured on the *Saturday Night Fever* soundtrack which I played regularly. I tuned in to hear the station's most popular deejay Paco Navarro's deep Puerto

Rican-accented baritone, and the mix of the disco tracks he played each afternoon enchanted me. I attended a 7th grade dance with my best approximation of John Travolta's disco suit: mine was white, with a mint green shirt.

I got a copy of the Third World album *96 Degrees In The Shade* as part of a grab bag at a classmate's birthday. The introduction to reggae was seismic. The prominent use of the bass and drums was reminiscent of my beloved disco and the lyrics took me right back to all the themes of the early 70s AM radio songs that had hit me so hard. They were seductive and meditative and helped me to disappear inside myself the same way I did in my parent's car listening to songs on the radio. And though I was too young to comprehend the full emotional and political weight of the songs, there was a haunting quality to the melodies and instrumentation that stayed with me. I played the album regularly, not fully aware it was called reggae, nor that the door to a new musical world had been opened.

America's slow burn of a love affair with the English Beat began in September 1980 when they were booked as the support act for a

three-month, coast-to-coast tour with their label mates the
Pretenders and Talking Heads. America and Americans initially
confused and confounded them and they endured severe culture
shock. According to Steele: *Furry armpits and sex – that's what the
average American think about.*[liii]

New York City circa 1980 was terrifying to them as well,
particularly to Wakeling who refused to leave his Upper West Side
hotel room while the band were in the city to play their American
debut:

> *The last time he stood in front of the Empire Hotel on 68th
> Street, a mammoth red fire truck roared past. Its screeching
> sirens and speed immediately made Dave panic – he threw
> himself against the side of a building. There was something
> about the people too – the way they stood so close, invading
> your personal zone, bearing down with harsh Brooklyn
> accents.*[liv]

Seymour Stein – a son of Brooklyn signed the band to Sire Records
in the US. Stein, a larger-than-life music executive, had been on a
shopping spree signing bands that would soon form the core of the
80s new wave era including the Ramones, and a young unknown
singer named Madonna. Stein, a self-confessed 2 Tone ska fan,
signed both Madness and the English Beat to Sire in the US,

believing he had a diamond in the rough with both bands. It's Stein
who paired the young band from Birmingham with the Pretenders
and Talking Heads noting:

> *The dark horse, however, proved to be the Beat, who nobody*
> *gave much attention to. They actually got signed from 2*
> *Tone to Arista's London office by a talented A&R man*
> *named Tarquin Gotch. Fortunately for me, he didn't make a*
> *strong enough case to Arista's head office in New York, who*
> *foolishly passed. I pounced on their North American rights*
> *and enjoyed both commercial success and many happy*
> *memories with the Beat, who we had to rebaptize the*
> *English Beat to avoid confusion with another group. We got*
> *them touring with Talking Heads and the Pretenders,*
> *almost double bills that never failed to blow away audiences*
> *everywhere they played. I really did enjoy that whole new-*
> *wave ska scene. Just a few bands made some of the hippest*
> *party music ever recorded.*[lv]

Roger remembered that though the Pretenders were all over
American radio at the time with "Brass In Pocket" and "Stop Your
Sobbing," the English Beat were punished for blowing them off the
stage each night:

After the third gig, their soundchecks began to take longer or would suspiciously start later. We then stopped getting soundchecks altogether. They did everything to make sure we had half lights, half the PA sound level, and people who got up to dance were sometimes thrown out during our second or third number. It was disheartening. [lvi]

Wright sensed a certain coldness from the Pretenders:

Funny, I don't remember so much about them and I don't have a good feeling about what I do remember particularly. [lvii]

The band had the opposite experience touring with Talking Heads who were warm and encouraging. According to Wright, the bands formed a mutual appreciation society:

There was a lot of close proximity between members of the bands. Several nights running in America after we'd been on stage and come off and toweled down a bit, Roger and I used to go out into the audience. And we just stood in the audience, well not stood, danced in the audience while Talking Heads were on, which was a lovely thing to be able to do. There were nearly always a couple of Talking Heads on stage wearing Beat t-shirts. We ended up staying in the same hotel as Talking Heads in LA. And Tina Weymouth presented me with a Talking Heads t-shirt that she said, "Well, I've just ironed this myself." I was enthralled by everything to do with Talking Heads. They were really tremendous as far as I was concerned. So to get a t-shirt from Tina Weymouth, I knew that was something I was never going to forget.[lviii]

Though the seven-man combo performed most shows without a soundcheck, they were so good that they were called back for encores from the sell-out crowds. Wakeling remembered Talking Heads fondly, the Pretenders not so much:

The gigs were a mixed bag. Supporting Talking Heads in Los Angeles and San Francisco was great; five chances to watch them closely on stage and staying in the same hotel as them we got to know them and become good friends. Supporting the Pretenders wasn't so much fun. No sound checks and their audience was much more of an "OK I've paid my money, entertain me" sort of crowd than we'd ever played to before. People who got up to dance were sometimes thrown out during our second or third number. Very depressing. We had to go back to a lot of cities and do a proper gig by ourselves, where people could dance if they wanted to, and weren't continually being pushed around by "tough guy" security men.[lix]

A *Sounds* profile from 1980 painted the scene of the band performing at the Greek Theatre in Los Angeles opening for Talking Heads:

Single male earrings jangling in the aisles, satin-jacketed execs kicking their Gucci boots up to their beards, journalists tapping their notebooks in time to contagious rhythms. The English Beat ("English" so as not to be confused with a similarly tagged quartet of mop top American Knack-sters) started the callouses forming with a hot set that belied reports of patchy live performances from earlier on this tour, and that managed to just about fit their entire repertoire into the short, allotted time.

The rhythm was spot on, the singing perfect and the sound so good it almost melted the speakers. A couple of minutes of pure beat burning into your brain then jaunting onto the next one, linked by some wild onstage bopping. 'Tears Of A Clown' stood out because just about everyone knew it. 'Mirror In The Bathroom' and 'Hands Off She's Mine' stood out because they're so damn good. A standing ovation, no less, brought them back for one more minute of 'Click Click' (openers just don't do encores at the Greek Theatres).[lx]

At one stop on the tour – Emerald City in Cherry Hill, NJ on October 10, 1980 – the band was filmed by Joe Massot for the cult ska documentary *Dance Craze* then capturing footage of all the 2 Tone era bands – the Specials, the Selecter, Madness and Bad Manners. *Dance Craze* later played as part of midnight shows at movie theatres in larger American cities and college towns and the soundtrack album from the film featuring "Mirror In The Bathroom," "Big Shot" and "Ranking Full Stop" further fueled the band's growing underground popularity with American audiences. Roger remembered the shoot:

> *While we were in the States, filmmaker Joe Massot had been travelling around the UK shooting footage of all the 2 Tone bands, including Bad Manners, who were seen as part of the whole ska revival. The film crew flew out to join us in Emerald City, Cherry Hill, New Jersey to record our set. It was a great gig and we finished off playing "Click Click" and "Jackpot" as an encore, but the audience kept on clapping and shouting for more. We had already played for an hour, so for a second time we went back on and played "Big Shot" and "Twist And Crawl". We were all saying, "Great! We're going to be in a movie.*[lxi]

Anecdotally, the Hooters, then a full-fledged ska band from across the Camden River in Philadelphia, opened the show. The Hooters keyboardist Rob Hyman became an instant fan:

> *We opened for the English Beat, who were another big influence, and then we hung out with them and we were drooling over their show because they just had it all. They had the toasting and the reggae and the rap and the rock, they really did it all.*[lxii]

After the initial success of the first US tour, the band spent the later part of 1981 and almost all of 1982 touring the US supporting the Clash and the Police. They become so much of an "it" band that Stein brought Madonna to one of the band's New York shows. The Material Girl was captivated:

> *The only things I ever did for Madonna was stuff like inviting her out to an English Beat gig, thinking she'd connect with their grooves and songwriting. Sure enough, her eyes and ears were glued to the stage all evening, and after the show, I took her backstage to meet Dave Wakeling, Ranking Roger and the other members of the band. I could tell she went home all fired up, realizing that dance music didn't have to be electronic and linear.* [lxiii]

Roger later revealed that he and Madonna were an item for a minute after they met:

> *Seymour Stein, the head of Sire Records, had introduced me to her in the States before she became a huge star. I found out she was a dancer at Danceteria, my favorite club in New York and I went to watch her a few times. Madonna was into the Beat and we chatted, had a couple of drinks together and got on. She was gorgeous but nothing happened. Then she came over to England to promote her debut single. After the performance I went back with her to her hotel. There was definitely a little twinkle in her eye. But I have to be truthful and say nothing more happened. We kissed outside her room and then I left.*[lxiv]

As the band crisscrossed America, the camaraderie of them all being in it together brought them closer, but also exposed some significant generational issues including meeting the needs of the nearly 60-year-old idiosyncratic Saxa and looking after a teenage Roger. Those duties often fell to Wright – a former social worker, who had a unique perspective on his bandmates. Of Saxa, Wright noted:

> *Saxa was overwhelmingly jovial and wonderful. He quickly became my buddy. As long as he was with the band he was*

my roommate. I can remember many times lying on our hotel beds in the middle of the night in America and Saxa would be munching on his chicken, which he liked to put on radiators to warm up a bit. He'd be eating his chicken and drinking a beer and I'd be lying on my bed having a smoke. And we used to spend half the night watching old movies on television.[lxv]

Wright also took on the role of serving as Roger's guardian on the road particularly during the early days of the band:

Roger was a babe in arms wasn't he? I mean, he was 16 when all this kicked off. My impression was how polite he was to everybody and how energetic he was, but we was very young. We had to go to magistrate's court before we went on several European and American tours in order to get permission to go because of Roger's age. It was all to do with making sure that young people are not exploited if they're working abroad. So I became, via the court like a guardian for the duration of the tour and to keep an eye on him. What was funny was that I was supposed to be making sure he was alright and some of the most beautiful women in Europe were lining up to lay themselves down in front of him! [lxvi]

While the band tour the country, my parents have finally ended their long-suffering marriage. My last memories of them together were of angry arguments and shouting about the fate of our family home as part of their pending separation. Though the recriminations faded once my father moved out, protesting loudly, *"I'm being kicked out of my own home,"* the ensuing silence and his absence left me feeling more alone and isolated. As such, I spent a lot of time alone in my room.

Now a single mother with two kids to feed, my mother took a low-paying office job that was a 30-minute commute from our house. Unfortunately, it took a heavy toll on her and she arrived home each night overwhelmed and cranky with the unrealistic expectation that Wendy and I have straightened up the house and started dinner. Life at home got substantially harder.

At 17, I was finally coming out of the vice-like grip of a terrible bout of ulcerative colitis that had dogged me on and off during the first two years of high school. Ulcerative colitis is a condition I would not wish on my worst enemy. Though I was familiar with the impact it had on Wendy who had been coping with it since she was 6 years old, nothing prepared me for having it myself.

Ulcerative colitis is a disease of the large intestine, in which the lining of the colon becomes inflamed and develops tiny open sores, or ulcers. It is as terrible as it sounds and its accompanied by painful diarrhea with blood and pus. I had come down with terrible, debilitating stomach cramps during and after coming home from a trip to the Philippines in August 1979 with my then best friend David and his family.

I had met David – a whip smart son of Filipino immigrants in sixth grade and we had become inseparable through much of middle school. We shared an interest in Monty Python, the Doctor Demento radio show, and popular music. He introduced me to Stevie Wonder's *Song's In The Key Of Life*, the Police, and the sounds of Black FM radio. I often slept over at his house, and we would stay up late and watch *Saturday Night Live*, then in its early days, read comic books and prank call girls from school. I was drawn to how independent he was and impressed that he was the family cook, preparing traditional Filipino meals for his family several nights a week. His family would often visit a cafeteria-style Filipino restaurant near the Lincoln Tunnel in Manhattan once a month and invited me to tag along. After a meal of pancit and adobo chicken, they would stop at a small Filipino grocery and stock up on staples including dried mango which I loved and *balut* (duck egg with embryo) which I did not.

In many ways a trip halfway around the world with my best friend during the summer of 1979 should have been the trip of a lifetime for a kid like me who was innately curious about the world. Little did I know how much that trip would change me for better and worse. Despite being surrounded by people nearly everywhere I went, it was my first time away from home and the first time I ever truly felt alone and on my own. To their credit, my parents agreed to let me go but I'm certain they desperately regretted their decision when I returned home much worse for wear.

Arriving in Manila after a nearly 24-hour flight with stops to refuel in San Francisco, Honolulu and Guam was eye opening, particularly the extraordinary blast of heat and humidity that hit me walking outside the airport terminal. The heat was a visceral punch to the gut and my senses. The drive from the airport to David's Uncle's compound in the upscale Makati section of the city stunned me. My eyes and brain were confronted by the chaos of traffic and ubiquitous Jeepneys – ornately decorated old American

Army jeeps that served as taxis and minibuses. More stinging was the street level poverty that overwhelmed my senses. Seeing the cruelty of the world just outside the window of the car seared my sensitive soul. It was all the sad stories of those 70's 45 singles coming to life.

Uncle's house was spacious and well-appointed and attended to by a small army of live-in maids and cooks. Uncle had some level of importance as an advisor to President Ferdinand Marcos, then at the height of his power. When we arrived, the Philippines was under martial law and in the throes of a political ideology known in Tagalog as *bagong lipunan* or "new society." Uncle's house was covered in the Marcos propaganda slogan, "*I'm proud to be a member of the new society.*" The idea was based on the ideology that Filipino society needed to be reformed and the only way that could happen was by placing it under the control of a benevolent dictator who could guide the undisciplined population through a period of chaos. There were large pictures of Marcos everywhere and his likeness even appeared on the five-peso coin.

Once we recuperated from the unrelenting jet leg, David's cousins took us on excursions to shops and malls around Makati. One memorable trip was to the Manila Polo Club – the premiere country club in the Philippines, established in 1909 during the American colonial era as a "home away from home" for American military officers and businessmen. The club retained a vaguely Eisenhower-era vibe, but instead of Americans with crewcuts, it served the cream of the crop of Filipino society and Marcos regime apparatchiks. I had a cheeseburger, french fries and a Coke while watching a polo match but it was hard to follow where the polo ball was amidst all the dust kicked up by galloping horses. I was gifted a Manila Polo Club t-shirt, which I never wore. The whole experience was disorienting.

I noticed I was having some stomach upset a few days after arriving, but David's mother – a nurse by training, chalked it up to crossing the date line and the local water. David's cousins were adamant about taking us out all over Manila, including bars and night clubs, where despite being only 14 years old, I was regularly offered bottles of San Miguel beer. It was clear that the good times were rolling for certain members of the New Society, and that bartenders didn't card underage minors in Manila. Despite the excitement of trying alcohol, my stomach upset continued and became a constant issue. I began feeling the urge to move my bowels on a regular basis and lost my appetite. No one seemed very concerned with my symptoms, so I tried to keep up with the busy schedule of sightseeing, visits to David's family across Manila and trips at night to get *Halo-Halo* – a layered dessert consisting of sweetened beans, fruits, shaved ice drizzled with evaporated milk, and ice cream.

We watched a lot of Filipino television, which was incomprehensible to me because it was all in Tagalog. But one show, featuring drag queens dancing and lip-synching to popular Filipino pop songs and standards, excited the entire household who gathered to watch, chattering and cheering for their favorites. *Everyone* laughed when I asked if these were real women and then when I confused the Tagalog words for *bakla* (gay) and *bulaklak* (flower).

David and I listened to a lot of Filipino radio which was obsessed with American disco and dance-oriented hits from recent American films like *Saturday Night Fever* and *Grease*. Evelyn Champagne King's song "Shame" was on constant rotation and played in every club we visit in Makati and young Filipinos were comparable to *Soul Train* dancers in their creativity and inventiveness. We visit a few record stores and buy compilation cassette tapes of popular disco songs then on Filipino radio. It's hard to fathom that just a few months later, in the fall of 1979, the world of music will change with releases by the Clash, the Specials, Madness and the Police.

David's family hailed from Zamboanga on the island of Mindanao, one of the southernmost cities in the archipelago of the Philippines. Located an hour and forty-five minutes south of Manila by plane, our visit there is a major part of the itinerary and everyone hopes it will be just the thing to snap me out of my lingering stomach ailment.

Spanish explorers, led by Ferdinand Magellan, arrived in the Philippine archipelago in 1521 and Zamboanga was chosen as the site of the Spanish settlement and garrison. Zamboanga – known as the City of Flowers becomes one of the main strongholds in Mindanao, supporting colonizing efforts on the island and making way for Christian settlements. It also served as a military outpost, protecting the island against foreign invaders. The city was occupied by the Japanese during World War Two but liberated by a mix of Filipino and American forces during a fierce battle in March 1945 as part of the effort to re-take Mindanao from Japanese control. As such, David's mother regaled me with tales about life during the Japanese occupation and how she cursed Japanese soldiers under her breath in Tagalog whenever she had to deal with them as a teenager during the war.

Martial law was in full effect in Zamboanga which was on the frontline of the Marcos regime's ongoing efforts to root out the Moro Islamic Liberation Front, an armed group seeking an autonomous region for the Moro people who were Muslims. There were Filipino soldiers at various check points throughout the city. Throughout the martial law years, more than a thousand citizens of Zamboanga are either killed, tortured, raped, or harassed by the Marcos government. As a result, there was a heavy vibe around the city and ongoing tension around impending Moro incursions.

David's family had a large home and compound located off a main boulevard near the center of the city. It looked like a more modern version of the Swiss Family Robinson house from the Disney movie. There was an open-air kitchen and limited plumbing, so all the water needed for cooking and bathing had to be boiled. Power brown outs were common during our stay and I was not prepared for the fact that the house had open windows and no air conditioning. We slept under mosquito netting. If urban Manila had been a culture shock, being in Zamboanga literally fried my brain.

Once we arrived, I was warned that as a *putting tao* or white person, I could be a potential target for Moro fighters who were periodically kidnapping and holding westerners for ransom. I was warned repeatedly not to leave the house or compound alone. At that point, my upset stomach had become nearly volcanic and I was relieved I could stay close to a bathroom. On the second or third day of our stay in Zamboanga and a week or so into the trip, I was hit by an intense wave of homesickness. I did my best to grit my teeth and endure but I was unprepared for how different everything was.

The sounds of Zamboanga attacked my suburban New Jersey sensibilities. Each morning around 3 or 4 am, roosters around the city began to crow loudly, in what sounded like a reggae sound clash battle. This made getting a solid night sleep impossible. The cacophony of pre-dawn roosters was compounded by the constant whine of mosquitoes that buzzed and divebomb the netting over my bed each night. The heat and humidity also made it hard to fall and stay asleep. The Filipino antidote to all this was *idlip* or a siesta, a holdover from Spanish rule. Around 2 or 3 pm each day, during the height of the heat, the whole city ate a large lunch and promptly went back to bed.

Sadly, my condition deteriorated and one night, overwhelmed by cramps and stomach pain, I noticed bright red blood in my stool. I gingerly woke David's mother and explained what had happened. She immediately got out of bed and made a phone call. Speaking rapidly in Tagalog, she arranged for me to see a doctor in the city center. Later that morning, I was taken in a Jeepney to see a General Practitioner who asked me a few questions and examined me before prescribing sleeping pills and small glass vials of liquid Vitamin B used to treat stress and anxiety.

Though the pills helped me to sleep, my stomach was still in turmoil and after several more bouts of blood, a decision was made to take me to a private hospital outside the Zamboanga city limits. I quickly packed a small bag and the whole family escorted me to my new residence.

I was given a private room with a bed, small armoire and window air conditioner. I was assessed by the doctor on call and then a young nurse who was assigned to care for me entered with a small white paper cup full of pills and watched me intently to make sure I took them all. She then informed me that an orderly would be arriving shortly to give me a suppository. Right on cue the orderly entered and did what he had to do. And so began several days of being confined to this room. I was served a breakfast of pasty oatmeal gruel and a lunch and dinner of plain white rice with white meat chicken or consommé. I'm not sure what medication I was given, but I slept like a rock and the unrelenting cramps abated for a bit.

David's mother stayed in the room with me for the first night and then came every few days to check on me. She let me know she had called my parents to let them know about me. Other than her visits, my only companions during this time were the young Filipina nurse and her co-workers who weren't much older than me and the slightly gruff orderly who dutifully visited each day bearing his small, oblong gift in a white paper cup.

The nurses were the first young women I had ever spent any time with outside of a few boy/girl middle school parties featuring spirited games of spin the bottle. The nurses all wore large Christian crosses and after asking if I had been born again, were surprised to learn I was a Jew. They continued to ask me about my relationship with Jesus Christ and seemed confused that I didn't consider him my Lord and savior. It was clear I was the first Jewish person they had ever met. Other than that, they mostly shared gossip with me about other patients they were caring for, including an old woman next door to my room, who, they offered with little explanation, was "going through a second childhood." I mostly passed the time either sleeping or reading a series of Filipino historical comic books that the nurses brought me that had a strong Christian point of view.

While I was in the hospital, David visited and shared the terrible news that New York Yankees catcher, Thurman Munson had died in a plane crash. Munson had been flying his Cessna Citation between New York and Canton, Ohio, where his family lived. His plane had crashed during a practice landing at the Akron-Canton Regional Airport. As a passionate fan of the team and of the swaggering Munson, I found the news difficult to comprehend in my medicated state.

After a week or so in the care of the young nurses, David's mother and the maids from the house came to collect me. Apparently, my unseen doctor had decided my treatment was complete and I was discharged. On the ride back to the compound, David's mother informed me we were heading back to Manila in the next two days.

But before we departed, a pig roast or *Lechon* was planned in my honor.

Lechon, derived from the Spanish word for roasted suckling pig, is one of the most popular dishes in the Philippines. The suckling pig is stuffed with lemongrass, tamarind, garlic, onions, and chives, and then roasted on a large bamboo spit over an open fire.

The preparation for the Lechon takes all day and I was asked if I wanted to participate in the slaughter of the pig. I politely declined, but later that night, as the banquet went into full swing under a brilliant night sky, I was presented with the pig's tail, which I was encouraged to eat. I did so. It was tough, stringy and sinewy. In retrospect, it may not have been the best thing to eat after getting out of the hospital with a sick stomach, but the overwhelming hospitality of David's extended family was heartwarming considering how homesick I was and how the accumulated trauma of being ill was catching up with me.

The lack of face time with David and my reliance on his mother had annoyed him. Apropos of nothing, the next morning, he announced with a flourish, "*Today, will be the worst day of your life,*" and with that stopped speaking to me and ignored me for the next few days.

The timing of his declaration came ahead of a trip to a small, tropical atoll, about an hour by boat from Zamboanga. The maids packed flatware, glasses and silverware for 20 people in large woven baskets and brought large metal pots of chicken adobo and rice which they heated over on open fire on the beach. Despite the silent treatment from David, the visceral experience of the gleaming blue water and pearly white sand was surreal. Adding to the stress of the occasion was the fact that the small island was within the area where Moro insurgents operated, so everyone made sure to remind me to stay close where they could keep an eye on me. We spent the day swimming in the water, eating, trying to climb coconut trees and sleeping on the beach.

We left for Manila the next day. And while David continued to give me the cold shoulder, his 17-year-old sister, who had ignored both of us for most of the trip, took pity on me and helped me to pack.

When we arrived back at Uncle's house in Manila, there was a letter from my mother. I'd briefly spoken to her after I was discharged from the hospital in Zamboanga and I kept up a brave face during the short international call. The truth was I didn't feel as well as everyone around me believed me to be. When I read my mother's letter, I was anxious to get home:

I was very happy to hear your voice and very relieved to know that you are on your way to a good recovery. You have certainly had some interesting experiences on your journey! I'm sure your hospital stay was very frightening. I know you will take this experience in your stride and it will serve you well in the future. I think you have handled it all very well.

And then just like that, the three of us – me, David and his sister – were on a plane from Manila to JFK Airport. We missed our connecting flight in Honolulu and had to spend the night at an airport hotel. Despite my weakened state, I was enchanted by the little I saw of Honolulu.

I arrived home in Princeton much worse for wear. The month away had whittled my weight down and my parents and my sister were visibly shaken by how skinny and tired I looked. I spent the next two days in a jet lagged stupor and then, without warning, my stomach revolted again. The symptoms I'd experienced in the Philippines had come back to torment me further. The only thing that made it bearable was that I was in my own home with my family.

I tried to resume my normal activities, including getting ready to go to my first year at Princeton High School, but I just didn't feel well. My parents, whose relationship seemed to have gotten worse while

I was gone, appeared overwhelmed by me and my symptoms. The final weeks of August and early September leading up to Labor Day were a blur of pain and discomfort. We visited my pediatrician who was concerned that I may have picked up a tropical bug while I was away.

On a follow-up visit to see the pediatrician the day or two before I was due for my first day of high school, he recommended we see a tropical disease specialist at Children's Hospital of Pennsylvania. During the long ride from Princeton to Philadelphia I was soothed by hearing new, exciting music on the radio by Prince, The Knack, and Chic.

After hearing about my symptoms and experience in the Philippines, the doctor recommended I immediately be admitted into an isolation ward so they could rule out any tropical diseases or illnesses I may have picked up on my travels. And so, began another hospital ordeal. The second in less than a month.

It's frightening to be ushered into a negative pressure room. These isolation rooms keep patients with infectious illnesses, or patients who are susceptible to infections apart from other patients, visitors, and healthcare staff. Instead of nervously riding my bike to the first day of high school, I was alone in an antiseptic room that felt like a prison cell.

The next few days featured people in masks, gowns and gloves poking and prodding me and taking more blood than it seemed possible I had in my veins. My parents visited but seemed powerless to do anything to help me. They were distraught and I felt utterly alone. I was placed on an IV and offered yellow, green or red Jell-O for all three meals for several days in a row. Adding to my misery was a Church's Fried Chicken restaurant I could see from the window of my hospital room. The inviting smell of the chicken as it was being cooked interrupted my all-Jell-O diet.

I endured several invasive colonoscopies with only slight sedation. They were incredibly unpleasant. The test results slowly trickled in. My blood work showed elevated white blood counts indicating some type of infection and the colonoscopies showed significant ulceration throughout my lower intestines.

Without warning, I was suddenly moved out of isolation into a regular room on a floor for sick teens. It was a relief to finally see the faces of my family and the doctors and nurses treating me. With some fanfare, one of the young doctors announced my diagnosis: ulcerative colitis. The plan was to keep me in the hospital until the steroids in my IV drip could reduce the inflammation that had invaded my digestive track. Though we now knew what we were dealing with given Wendy's previous diagnosis,

I was still wracked with pain. And so, I spent nearly the entire month of September 1979 in a hospital bed.

At first my mother and father visited regularly and then just my mother who stayed overnight with me, sleeping on a small cot the hospital provided. It was clear that my illness was having a profound effect on her when one evening as we are getting ready to go to sleep, she began to have a terrible migraine and then vomited non-stop. As I sat and watched in disbelief, the nursing staff assessed her, noting her blood pressure was through the roof. They quickly called for an ambulance. Within minutes, a crew of EMTs entered the room, moved her on to a stretcher and whisked her off to a local ER that treated adult patients. I did not see my mother or father again for several days.

Though I spoke with my parents on the phone, I was essentially on my own in the hospital for a week or so. That time alone intensified the stoicism I've had since I was young, and that has stayed with me the rest of my life. I watched TV, listened to a small transistor radio my parents brought me and looked out the window.

Once it was determined that my ulcerative colitis was responding to the high doses of steroids in my IV, I was discharged and bid a hasty farewell to Children's Hospital of Pennsylvania and Philadelphia. I returned home to my own bedroom but felt completely dislocated from time and space. Though I'd been away for most of the summer and had missed the first month of high school, it was decided I needed another two weeks at home to recuperate. As I got my strength back, a teacher visited me at home with assignments and made a lackluster attempt to get me ready for in person high school.

I finally begin high school in mid-October 1979 and immediately felt like an outsider. I was not prepared for the hustle and bustle of the hallways between classes and the huge cafeteria was intimidating. Despite having gone to middle school with all my 9th grade classmates, I felt like a new student and repeatedly answered questions about what was wrong with me and where I'd been.

During this time my parents made a feeble attempt to hold it together, but shortly after my return to school, they were back to arguing at full volume leaving me feeling sorry for myself in my bedroom. Ulcerative colitis is often the result of the immune system's overactive response. My immune systems' overactive response was likely caused by the constant stress and discord in my home and the lingering unhappiness that had hung over it for several years like a low, dense fog.

It was during this time, when any joy I had seemed to have
vanished, that music, specifically the Specials and 2 Tone suddenly
appeared, like a life preserver on stormy seas. David who had
studiously avoided me since our return home – I assumed out of
embarrassment for how he had treated me in the Philippines,
redeemed himself by lending me a copy of the Specials self-titled
debut album. His parents had enrolled him at the Lawrenceville
School, a prestigious private school near Princeton and he was now
living in a dorm with classmates from all over the world who were
in the know about all the latest music trends.

On a visit to see him at his new school, David played the record for
me in his dorm room, I had an immediate lightning bolt moment.
The combination of punk and ska was jarring and unlike anything
I'd ever heard in my young life. The lyrics, sung by Terry Hall in
an insistent, angry and annoyed tone were mostly indecipherable.
But the questioning of authority and the messages of unity
resonated with me immediately. And though I heard some
similarities to my Third World album, this was something
altogether different. As I listened, a switch in my brain flipped on
and I was flooded with a familiar warm feeling from the days of

listening to AM radio in the car. I felt connected to something much larger than myself and I felt transported spiritually.

While the music was mesmerizing, the album art was just as powerful. A gang of seven men – five white and two Black – stared out at me with intent. They looked angry, as if they were looking for a fight. And yet, there was an urgency to their message of calling out the crazy world around them that I needed to hear. *Curtain has fallen, now you're on your own/I won't return, forever you will wait* Hall intoned in "You're Wondering Now." It sounded simultaneously joyful and angry; hopeless and idealistic, nostalgic and innovative. It was everything I was feeling as a lonely teen searching for an identity, in the very fucked-up world around me.

And though music and the radio had always played a big part of my inner world, this was something far bigger and more important. I suddenly had a critical mission: find more music that sounded like the Specials! As I began to feel better, I started to have some semblance of a "normal," early 80s, teenage experience. Though there was no sex or drugs (except for the massive dose of prednisone I took daily to treat the inflammation of my ulcerative colitis), there would soon be plenty of rock and roll.

Although I had discovered a portal to a new world of music, the next two and a half years of high school were challenging. My experience with ulcerative colitis had made me an introverted loner. I did fairly well in my classes, since I tended to go directly home after school and do my homework, but I was soon making regular stops at the Music Cellar. My visits there began to open up a whole new world of music that spoke to me in ways the corporate pop and rock music on commercial AM and FM radio did not.

One afternoon after school in late May of 1980, while perusing the aisles of the Music Cellar, I worked up the nerve to speak to one of the record store clerks behind the counter. I generally found the clerks intimidating and judgmental, but I mentioned I had the Specials album and asked if he could recommend anything else like it. His smile immediately put me at ease: "The Specials are great but check out the English Beat who are just as good and have just released a new album." I quickly made my way to the E section and there in all its pink and black pop art glory was *I Just Can't Stop It.*

Listening to that record soon became one of the great pleasures of my life and I quickly memorized the track order and most of the lyrics – or at least those that I could understand. If the Specials were looking for meaning in the black and white of life, the English Beat found musical meaning in vivid technicolor. And though I had not yet decided I wanted to play the bass, I was drawn to the relentless sound of the rhythm section. Steele and Morton combined to propel the songs forward with a unique combination of furious bass notes and insistent rim clicks that were soon buried within my subconscious. According to Wakeling, Steele's bass lines may have been the band's secret weapon:

David Steele was the Mozart of the bass, a taciturn genius of the time and very affable. He started playing things on the bass guitar that none of us had ever heard of before. The first band that he'd been in had two bass players and a drummer. One bass player played really low and he would play the melodies really high. When we would start rehearsing, he would start out with a typical bass guitar line, and about three minutes in, he would play the melody. We had to sort that so he could keep the bass going. He went on to be the genius behind the Fine Young Cannibals as well, a talented lad. On some songs, we would just let him come up with a bass line, and it was our job to figure the rest out. Other times, the bassline could come quite a long way into the songs; the other instruments are making a dominating pulse, and all of a sudden, the bassline appears. It worked in different ways, really.[lxvii]

Wright was struck by Morton's unorthodox approach to playing the drums – employing rim shots where you would expect to hear the snare:

> *And I'm listening one day at soundcheck and Everett was up on stage, and I was out front, and the sound man said, "Listen to Everett. When he does that, people want to dance." And that was it. There's a lightness, a springiness of touch to his drumming, which is a reflection of his character and personality.*[lxviii]

The uniqueness of the band's sound may have been a happy accident, having much to do with how differently Morton and Steele – both self-taught musicians -- approached their instruments. According to Wakeling:

> *David Steele was a punk with a clear idea of what he wanted and where he was going. Everett Morton was a left-handed drummer; he had his kit set up like a right-handed drummer but played it left-handed. His was an original style and if you worked with it, it sounded real unique.*[lxix]

According to Steele, much of the credit for solidifying the sound of the band was a direct result of Morton joining the band: *It gave us a real reggae influence, which before we had just talked about.*[lxx]

109

Wakeling agreed, noting *Everett's prior experience in soul bands helped forge the bridge between the various styles and influences.*[lxxi]

Though I loved *I Just Can't Stop It* LP, I was drawn back again and again to "Tears of a Clown," a song that spoke directly to me as I tried to grin and bear my way through health trauma and familial trials and tribulations. As it turned out, the inclusion of the song on the album – which went to number 6 on the UK singles chart was the song that brought the band together. It was a song played out of necessity for band members still learning how to play together. According to Wakeling the song was a happy accident:

> When we were rehearsing the songs, we'd sound great for a minute or two then we'd all veer off into our own personal visions of the song then it'd become a cacophony again, then it would all veer back for another minute or two and it would sound wonderful. Just the right amount of balance and tension.

The drummer, Everett, said, "Why don't we all try and learn to play a song that we all know already, know how to play and then we can go back to your weird ones like that mirror song." It took us quite a long time to think of a song because we were not a peer group but after about ten minutes of shouting out song titles everyone knew 'Tears Of A Clown'. Well we said knew it, but it turns out we didn't really know the chords to it, but we knew some of them... most of them. Andy eventually learnt the chords, which helped a lot. So, we would practice 'Tears Of A Clown', then we'd practice 'Mirror In The Bathroom', 'Tears Of A Clown', 'Twist And Crawl', 'Tears Of A Clown', 'Click Click', 'Tears Of A Clown', 'Big Shot', 'Tears Of A Clown', 'Two Swords' etc.

So, every practice, we'd end up playing 'Tears Of A Clown' a lot more than any of the other songs and eventually, we had 7 songs. David Steele who was the punk translator because he was 19, coming on 20 and Andy and I were now 21, and you weren't allowed to be a punk if you were over 21. But we were 20 for the first two months of '77 so we were, 'in,' the club and we worked on the basis that once you were in then you were in the club and that was it; you weren't kicked out of it after your first birthday.

*Anyway, David said you only needed 8 songs to do a show
and we had 7 so we decided to put 'Tears Of A Clown' in. We
played everywhere we could: punk shows, reggae shows,
working men's clubs, parties for old ages pensioners who
used to work at factories and their grandchildren. Some
songs that would go down great and some songs not so good,
but it didn't matter who the crowd was, 'Tears Of A Clown'
always went down. "Fantastic," they said, "Fantastic."* lxxii

The other song on the album that absolutely mesmerized me was
"Mirror In The Bathroom." The hypnotic bass and drums and the
bracing lyrics transported me each time I listened. I'd spent a lot of
time staring in the mirror at the contours of my prednisone-shaped
moon face which contrasted with my skin and bones physique, and
the song captured the angst and moodiness I was feeling from the
side effects of the medication and from puberty. I hardly recognized
myself. As it turned out, the inspiration for the song came from a
similarly uncomfortable one-on-one experience that Wakeling had
with his own reflection:

*I was working in construction at the time, and it was the
winter, I had forgotten to hang my jeans up to dry overnight,
so when I got into the bathroom to shower up, I noticed my
jeans were still on the floor, soaking wet, covered in sand.
So, I hung them up thinking well, it's probably best to have*

them steaming hot and wet. I went to shave, and it was snowing, and I really, really didn't want to go. So, I started talking to myself in the mirror as I was shaving up. And it was weird, because I looked deeper in the mirror, and I could see the little caption on the door behind, and I said to myself, Look, David, there's just me and you in here. The door's locked. We don't have to go to work.

Of course, we did. Got on the motorbike, and I just started pondering as I skated my way to the construction site on this motorbike. And that's how it started. It was thinking about how self-involvement turns into narcissism and how narcissism turns into isolation, and then how isolation turns into self-involvement again, and how what a vicious cycle that can become. So then I just started thinking about different situations where people would ostensibly look like they were doing something, but in fact they were checking their own reflection out. And you'd see it perhaps on Saturday afternoon with people window shopping, half the time they're actually just looking at their own reflection. Then this restaurant opened, and it was a big deal at the time because it had glass tables, and I was like, oh, you can watch yourself. [lxxiii]

I Just Can't Stop It became a constant companion that year. I played it so much that Wendy often hid the record from me because she was tired of hearing it.

In the spring of my Sophomore year in 1981, the band released their follow-up, *Wha'ppen*, which was a Jamaican phrase that Roger used regularly which translated as "What's going on?" Just as I was getting acclimated to the speedy punk meets reggae of their first LP, the band abruptly zig zagged, drawing in an array of new influences including African, steel band and dub reggae. According to Roger, the new album was a huge departure even for the band members themselves:

> *That album was weird because the first album was really up and dancey and then that album was more relaxed, and I don't know what people thought, but when it came out people were like, 'what's happened to the Beat?.* [lxxiv]

Lyrically, *Wha'ppen* was as strong as the band's debut and often stronger. While the music lacked the buzz that came on so strong on *I Just Can't Stop It* where songs collided into each other at dizzying tempos, the new songs were more cohesive and pointedly

114

anti-racist, anti-military and anti-capitalist. Like the Specials *More Specials* album, *Wha'ppen* required multiple listens to appreciate its offerings. Distinct changes were taking place song to song: a blast of brass here, a steel drum there, odd percussion throughout (including garden shears!). The band were clearly in uncharted waters musically.

And while there were musical subtleties, the lyrics were notable for their bold shift to documenting the new realities of life in Margaret Thatcher's England: "Cheated" was an articulate condemnation of early 80s UK right wing media like *The Sun* newspaper that sought to distract and separate with lines like: "*We're reading tissue paper but we can talk about real things later.*" There was also a passionate anti-nuclear war song, "Dream Home in New Zealand" that featured the eerie sound of whales as it noted the way the Cold War was bringing the world to the brink of a nervous breakdown; the anti-war song "I Am Your Flag" about the effects of the war machine on soldiers in conflicts in Northern Ireland, Afghanistan and the Middle East; there were warnings over the destructive role of officially sanctioned government violence in "Over and Over" and the brutal impact of economic deprivation on the working class in "The Limits We Set" with its repeated chant of "shoplifting." These were not trite slogans but warnings in real time from the front lines of life in cities across Britain that were struggling.

Cox weighed in on his approach to the new songs during an interview with the *Baltimore Sun* in 1982:

> *The advantage of a multiracial band is you get a big spread of influences, because everyone has different backgrounds. For example, the kind of music that Roger would put on the cassette deck in the van is not the same thing I would tape at home, because I don't have the same records. So you hear a lot of things you wouldn't have heard otherwise. And it comes out in the way you play. I think we went over the top a bit with Wha'ppen, but it's better to do that than to avoid politics completely.* lxxv

According to Roger, the change in direction was driven by 80s era experimentation as well as a note from an American fan pleading with the band to slow down their tempos:

> *On the first album when we were on the Beat bus we used to listen to a lot of reggae, a lot of punk y'know like Devo, the Clash and people like that. It was very exciting, a nice mesh of music but when the guys felt like they'd had enough dub stuff cause the bass was too heavy and they'd had enough of the punk stuff because it was too thrashy we needed something a bit more mellow. We started listening to loads of West African music so you can hear that influence. So,*

what you listen to on your bus could dictate what your next album sounds like.

So, we took some time off after touring with the Pretenders and started jamming again. Within it all we'd been reading our fan club letters and we got this one from a lady in America saying I've tried to use your music for my keep fit lessons and it's too fast. It was a lovely written letter, so we decided to tone it down a bit in the way that the Beat became what we call 'one-drop', where the rim shot and the snare hits at the same time and that's the main emphasis. So, we did "Doors of your Heart" and "Monkey Murders" and along with a few others and that was the kind of style for that album in the end.

But it was difficult because we had to come up with tunes, so what we were doing on tour was we had a notepad each and we'd keep them for two or three days and then pass them on to the next person.

Everybody would write onto somebody else's thing and a lot of the lyrics from the second album and the third album came in that way. It was a great way to get stuff together and say well that's a band effort. Cause even like the smallest line from the drummer could get into the song. We

used a lot of bits from headlines and stuff like that. It all
came together and made sense. So that took a while to
record and get right but when it did come out in England it
was met with mixed reactions. A lot of people were like well
it's not ska is it? You've done like the Specials and mellowed
out or whatever it is. But in California all of a sudden, all
the surfers and beach bums, the mods out there, we'd go out
there and they'd be lapping it up. That's when I realized how
brilliant this band was at merging in such a subtle,
sophisticated way and not in a pushing it in your face way.
lxxvi

I'd spend mornings before my first period class in the high school library perusing the weekly copy of the *Village Voice*. Robert Christgau's succinct and fragmented reviews helped guide me and informed my list of future purchases at the Music Cellar. He gave *Wha'ppen* and its more diverse rhythms an A, noting:

David Wakeling shows more character (and timbre) than
Terry Hall, Ranking Roger could rub his dub in a pedigreed
reggae band, and the rhythms aren't solely riddims. So as
two-tone grays out, the Beat follow their chops into the
world-beat sweepstakes, where snaky grooves are worth
their weight in yen. The Afrobeats and studio spaces and
steel drums are as seamlessly colloquial as the depression

118

politics and depressed romances, so it would be a shame if its sinuous midtempos dismay fans of its predecessor's hectic pace. I hear not resignation or compromise but a stubborn, animated adaptability. Unity rocker: "Doors of Your Heart," in which love means eros and agape simultaneously, and Wakeling finds that dread blocks the way to both, and Roger advises him to stop his fighting. lxxvii

Listening to *Wha'ppen* was like an audio encyclopedia that opened a door into the adult world of global politics and failing interpersonal relationships that I was all too familiar with. The songs were bleak but offered glimmers of hope with memorable melodies and hooks. The companion album art was designed by the brilliant cult cartoonist and artist Hunt Emerson, who had created the iconic Beat girl that graced the first album cover and countless t-shirts. Emerson's mural of the band which was used for the cover art is the antithesis of *I Just Can't Stop It*, featuring a colorful portrait of the band set against a large, looming tidal wave. According to Emerson, the design was a last-minute creation:

I did a small painting of Dave, Everett and David. They liked the idea so I went back to Birmingham to see what I could make of it. I sat down late one Sunday evening to idly sketch a few thoughts, and 36 hours later I done this huge painting, the glaring hard acrylic paints squeezed straight

119

from the tube in some parts. And there was a psychedelic
tidal wave in the background. They kept saying things about
a tidal wave. The whole recording an album process was like
a tidal wave. That was it. [lxxviii]

As it turns out, "Drowning" from *Wha'ppen* with its slow, dark and
downbeat reggae captured my teenage mindset ("*So in between the*
sleepless nights/You dream that you are winning fights/But then it
happens, dreadful thing/A wave appears too big to swim/You're
drowning, you're drowning..."). Though I associated the song with
my own personal drama at the time, it turned out to be a veiled
swipe at Sire Records and presumably Seymour Stein. According to
Wakeling:

> *The song was about our first disenchantment with the*
> *record industry. We were disappointed with the attention we*
> *got from our label, since they had the Pretenders, Talking*
> *Heads and Madness, and we seemed to slip between the*
> *cracks. So when we went to New York, the label wanted to*
> *take us out to dinner, and I was too embarrassed. I wouldn't*
> *go. They kept sending people up to the room, and I kept*
> *saying I wasn't going. I sat and mused upon it, and I felt like*
> *I was drowning, and that's how the song was born. I also*
> *think it was the first pop song with whale noises in it. We*
> *mixed a few of those in there.* [lxxix]

I could relate. Life at home felt like a ship on rough seas. I innately sensed my mother was doing her best given the circumstances. Like a ship's captain trying to navigate without a map during a sudden storm, she was lost at sea. As such, my family was being tossed wildly by the waves of life. *Wha'ppen* captured this queasy time for me, my family and many others during the Thatcher and Reagan years. A review of the album by Milo Miles in *Rolling Stone* magazine on its release in October 1981 summed up how the band captured the ups and downs of modern life during the early 80s:

> Wha'ppen *asks the right questions: what are the fears tearing daily life apart? What are the tactics, however brutal, that everyone uses to cope? And by thinking in terms of a whole record, the English Beat leave themselves room to build suspense and plant their depth charges.* [lxxx]

As Roger stated succinctly in an interview about *Wha'ppen* with The Quietus in 2012: *The music was happy, the lyrics sad. We always had a yin-yang thing going.* [lxxxi]

Issues with Sire Records had been on steady boil for some time and the band was considering a change ahead of the release of *Wha'ppen*. Before the band's third British tour, Cox travelled to New York to meet Clive Davis who wanted to convince the band to release Wha'ppen in the U.S. on the Arista label instead of on Sire Records.

> *Andy had already met with other record company officials*
> *who warned him, "We stop at nothing and stoop to*
> *everything – don't fuck up, kid. Don't fuck up." But Davis*
> *was more refined in his lilac Barry Manilow tour jacket,*
> *deep in the heart of Manhattan's corporate music business.*
> *He explained to Andy that while "Doors of Your Heart" could*
> *easily break America, Beat lyrics were too "socially aware,"*
> *which might "threaten" US audiences. Maybe it was the tour*
> *jacket, but Wha'ppen was eventually released on Sire by*
> *default.*[lxxxii]

At the end of 1981, the band had more commercial success with the album peaking at number 3 on the UK albums chart.
NME ranked *Wha'ppen?* at No. 4 on their top ten "Albums of the Year" while Hot Press named it the 15th best album of 1981. In the US, the album ranked at No. 23 on the 1981 Pazz & Jop' critics poll of the year's best albums. Robert Christgau, who curated the poll, ranked it at No. 5 on his personal "Dean's List" of the best albums of the year.

Despite a glowing review of *Wha'ppen* in 1981, *The Record Mirror* reviewer raised questions about the band's pending third album:

I'm not going to judge this record too early – the Beat don't grab, they suggest. But already I'm aware how well mixed the Beat are. The first Beat album depended on good songs and separate skills. Separate skills become unity rockers here. Whether the next record will suffer from such cohesion is an open question, but right now, the Beat goes on.[lxxxiii]

With two critically acclaimed albums on the radar of music critics, radio DJs and a growing American fanbase, the band were wrestling with two main issues: finding a new record label that could help them market their sound– perhaps a middle ground between their two albums – and how best to unlock the key to success in America.

A year later, perhaps with Clive Davis' advice to Cox still ringing in their ears, Steele teased the band's new direction while previewing tracks from the as yet untitled third album during an interview on KTRU-FM, the Rice University college radio station during July 1982:

We've gone totally into love songs. We've given up politics. In England people stopped asking about music completely. They just want to know our opinion on what's happening in South America, or Northern Ireland or England. So this album is not so political. [lxxxiv]

By the summer of 1982, with the help of the English Beat, I'm finally feeling more like myself. Music was important medicine during this time. It gave me an identity, a reason for living and was my best friend. Albums and liner notes became sacred texts I studied daily and trips to the Music Cellar after school and over summer break were visits to a holy shrine where I discovered new music that sustained me and opened my mind to ideas of love, political protest, relationships, sex and the confusion of adult life. I soon added albums from the entire 2 Tone canon to my collection: The Selecter, Madness, and Bad Manners, as well as British reggae by UB40 and Steel Pulse and new wave music by the Smiths, Echo & The Bunnymen, Depeche Mode, Devo and B-52s. Despite the much-needed musical distraction, fate had more trials and tribulations in store for me.

October 1, 1982

"I don't know how I'm meant to act with all of you lot, sometimes I don't try."

-- Save It For Later

As the English Beat and I.R.S. were preparing to release *Special Beat Service* and to conquer America during the Fall of 1982, I started my senior year at Princeton High School, buoyed by music and a loose group of friends I had slowly made over the previous year. Some were middle school acquaintances and others were new friends of friend's, but for the most part they were a boisterous and rowdy group of WASPY teenage boys into sports and music. Jokes, particularly making fun of people was their currency and I had to be careful and watch my step around them. I was innately aware that they wouldn't tolerate anything that smacked of weakness or sensitivity. I was initially included in their rough after-school games of tackle football and 3 on 3 basketball and held my own despite occasional verbal cheap shots to test my mettle and to prove I wasn't a "pussy."

The group were also fans of Strat-O-Matic sports boardgames and that fall we started a Strat-O-Matic club which allowed us to play games in an empty classroom after school. For the uninitiated, in the days before the advent of video game consoles, Strat-O-Matic allowed passionate sports fans to use player cards that reflected the player's real-life statistics and dice to replicate real game play. Our games were loud and full of trash talk and though I had fun playing, unlike others in the club, I didn't take the wins and losses all that seriously. And that made one of the leaders of the group who was a sore loser, very annoyed with me.

I enjoyed being part of a peer group but my place in the hierarchy felt tenuous and I was often the butt of jokes prompted by any ideas I had that didn't align with their conservative political world view which was now all the rage thanks to Ronald Reagan. In middle school the sore loser had stolen one of my notebooks that I had put anti-nuclear power stickers on. He defaced it by crossing out the stickers with dark blue ink and writing "We need it" all over the cover. After searching for my notebook, I finally found it in a garbage can in the school gym. I never mentioned it to anyone, but I was very wary of him.

At that point in my AP American history class we were studying Prohibition and our teacher mentioned the famous 1920s-era gangster Hymie Weiss, a Polish Catholic mob boss who was the leader of the North Side Gang in Chicago and a bitter rival of Al Capone. Weiss was known as *'the only man Al Capone feared.'* I'm not sure how the tide turned, but suddenly, later that fall I became regular fodder for the group's teasing which focused on Weiss.

Despite the fact that Weiss was not Jewish, outside of class this group of boys started to call me "Hymie Weiss." Hymie is derived from the Hebrew word *Chaim* ("Life") and the "Hymie" moniker would soon be in the news a year or so later. During an interview with the *Washington Post* in 1984, the Rev. Jesse Jackson, who was running for President, referred to Jews as "Hymies" and New York City as "Hymietown." It goes without saying that "Hymie" was an ethnic slur for Jews, and the casual use of it by these boys both terrified and infuriated me.

What started as cruel teasing quickly escalated to daily bullying. The more I protested the slur, the more the bullying intensified. These boys soon got other people in school to call me Hymie which made it far worse. I distanced myself from the group and quit the Strat-O-Matic club which angered and then emboldened them further. Ahead of history class one day, they taped a crude Nazi-era, anti-Semitic cartoon of a Jew with exaggerated features including a large nose, beady eyes, a beard and yarmulke to my desk and laughed at my reaction when I walked in, saw it and ripped it up. The angrier my responses the more they reveled in taunting me. The negative attention made it nearly impossible for me to focus during class and I dreaded going to school.

It's hard to describe my mindset during this time, but I felt isolated and vulnerable. Many times, during those fall months, I had an overriding sense that there was no escape from what was happening. I'd lived inside my own head for much of my life, but this was unbearable. I did my best to be stoic and impassive like I had been in the hospital a few years earlier, but I feel besieged.

It got worse. One of the boys –the sore loser who had defaced my notebook, had gotten my locker combination. One morning, as I opened my locker before school, I was confronted by a large picture of Yasir Arafat – then the leader of the Palestine Liberation Organization that had been taped to the inside of the locker door. A line had been crossed and I was overcome with anger and humiliation. I felt violated and I finally broke down and told my mother what had been going on.

My mother had been going through her own personal issues that were having an impact of her blood pressure and her mental health. Ironically, she was trying to make a living as a low-level employee at a company that manufactured and marketed blood pressure monitors. She hated the job and returned home from work each night depleted and frustrated. She had been inattentive to what was happening with me and Wendy, who was a precocious ninth grader and running with a hard partying group of older kids.

The news of my bullying was a shock back to reality for my mother. She was angry when I explained what had happened and asked me over and over why I hadn't told her sooner. But she suddenly seemed determined to end my suffering in a way she couldn't when I was sick in the Philippines or hospitalized in Philadelphia.

Despite my protests, she called the high school principal. He put an end to the bullying by calling the parents of several of the boys involved, but not before making me and the two ring leaders of the bullying sit in his office for an extremely awkward meeting where he tried unsuccessfully to draw us out. I stared at the floor the entire time to avoid the faces of my tormentors.

My mother also called the mothers of the two ring leaders to tell them what had been going on. The meeting in the principal's office and my mother's phone calls had the desired effect: the bullying finally ended. But socially, as far as this group was concerned, I no longer existed. I was *persona non grata*. As a final, cruel parting gesture, several of them added "Heimy" to their high school yearbook picture descriptions. It was one last humiliating inside joke they could bond over about the glory days of high school when they tormented me. It made it difficult for me to even look at the yearbook for many years afterwards.

Right on schedule and to my psychic rescue, enter the English Beat, who had just released their third album *Special Beat Service* in the US on Friday October 1, 1982. A review in the October 2, 1982 issue of the *Record Mirror* teased what was in store:

> *Those of you who wrote off the Beat after* Wha'ppen *prepare to eat your words. More concise, more structured, more melodic, more punchy, more romantic, more cynical, more or less the most brilliant album of 1982.* Special Beat Service *re-affirms the Beat are one of Britain's best bands.* [lxxxv]

As I held the *Special Beat Service* album in my hands that unseasonably warm autumn day outside the Music Cellar, I was hypnotized by the cover art. The photo – taken by noted rock photographer Bruce Fleming (who shot Jimi Hendrix's first LP cover *Are You Experienced*) captured what appeared to be a Middle Eastern dignitary of some importance (played by Saxa) deplaning from a British Air Super VC-10 aircraft while being protected by a security detail made up of the rest of the band. I asked myself, "what exactly is going on in this picture? What does the album cover mean?" I immediately noticed that the Beat girl featured on *I Just Can't Stop It* had been replaced by a new wave-like logo of an airplane. I raced home on my bike to listen and ponder the cover art's symbolism.

To my 17-year-old sensibilities, the *Special Beat Service* moniker sounded cool even if I didn't know what it meant I didn't learn until much later that the album title was a reference to the Falkland Islands conflict.

In April 1982, the Falklands War, a ten-week undeclared war between Argentina and England, began when Argentine military forces invaded the islands (which the Argentines called by their Spanish name: Islas Malvinas) and other British territories in the South Atlantic, briefly occupying them until that June when a British expeditionary force retook the territories by force. Patriotic sentiment was high in Argentina at the beginning of the conflict, but the unfavorable outcome prompted large protests against the ruling military government, hastening its downfall. In the UK, the Conservative Thatcher government, bolstered by the successful outcome, was re-elected with an increased majority in Parliament the following year.

The conflict had a social and cultural impact on both countries and became the source for various books, articles, and films. In England, it spurred a number of leading British musicians including New Order (Love Vigilantes), Elvis Costello ("Shipbuilding"), Big Country ("Fields of Fire") and The Fixx ("Liner") to reference the war in songs released after the end of the conflict. As it turned out, *Special Beat Service* was a play on the

131

Special Boat Service, a British special forces unit established after World War Two. According to Roger:

> *It was also the name of the of the first unit to be dispatched to the Falkland Islands during the conflict in 1982 and I have a memory of us all listening to a debate in the House of Commons about the war while we were recording the album. For Margaret Thatcher, the conflict would help to propel her and the Conservatives to a second landslide general election victory the following year. For the Beat, the new album was an opportunity to cross over to a mainstream audience and potentially conquer the American market.*[lxxxvi]

I devoured the album and played it three or four times in a row that afternoon while I scoured the lyric sheet and liner notes for clues.

Special Beat Service came out over a year after *Wha'ppen* was released and the band had taken more time in preparing for its recording and production. Wakeling shared during an interview with *Trouser Press* in late 1982, the care taken during pre-production for their third release:

> *We played it really carefully with this one. In January we*
> *were working with 18 unfinished songs which we slowly*
> *whittled down to 12. We stripped bits from the songs we*
> *dropped and put them into the 12 we wanted. We wanted to*
> *make sure this was a good one, because its either our first*
> *international album or the last Beat album.*[lxxxvii]

The album was recorded at Roundhouse Recording studios in the
Camden section of London with Sargeant at the helm again. At the
time, Roundhouse was the premiere studio in London and the first
digital studio in the world. Artists as diverse as Kajagoogoo,
Queen, Motorhead, Haircut One Hundred and AC/DC recorded
there. But the English Beat, who were returning for a third time,
made history by being the first band to use its digital recording
capabilities for the recording of "Mirror In The Bathroom" as the
first digital single and *I Just Can't Stop It* as the first digital
album.

Leading up to the recording of *Special Beat Service*, some members
of the band got together to work on new songs. According to Wright:

> *I remember there were some occasions every now and then,*
> *when Shuffle and Everett would shut themselves away for*
> *an afternoon messing around with various rhythm ideas and*
> *sometimes I'd join on piano. The bulk of the lyrics came from*

Dave and he was very encouraging of others in the band to come up with lyrics. At one point, we all had little notebooks we carried around. The idea being that anybody could jot down little sentences and ideas.[lxxxviii]

Before entering the studio to record *Special Beat Service*, the band lived together in a house in London where they spent time in pre-production writing and revising three songs a day. According to Wakleing, the process of recording the third album focused on creating space within the songs. They had a small TEAC portable studio which they used to record demos and then later shared with Sargeant who suggested new ideas and modifications. According to Roger: *Bob always kept it interesting. He would always say, "Try another style." He would encourage you to try things.* [lxxxix]

Based on Sargeant's feedback the band made changes, played through new versions of the songs and developed lyrics. Sargeant was a moderating influence on the band, bringing a sense of discipline and, most importantly, a willingness to say "No" to some of the band members' more wildly creative ideas. This ultimately resulted in a timeless quality to their recorded output. According to Wakeling:

I think there's two main reasons the music has lasted. One's just audio. That Bob Sargeant, our producer, wouldn't allow

us to use any of whatever had just been invented in terms of
synthesizers. And we had some people in the band who
would've liked to have done. But for the main part, the songs
are drums, bass, two guitars, maybe some keyboards, some
saxophone, some tambourine. If you wanted string sounds,
it'd have to be a string quartet from the Royal Philharmonic.
If you wanted a piano, it'd have to be a Steinway grand,
miked with a rhythm mic at just the correct angle as per the
BBC handbook.[xc]

Wright noted that Sargeant was an affable and friendly guy who
was able to get the best out of people but would not abide any
synthesizers: "*So by the end of the sessions, I'd played pianos and a*
bit of Hammond organ, and a bit of Vox Continental organ, but
never a synthesizer."[xci] Wakeling noted that during his time at the
BBC, Sargeant was trained by the book how to properly record a
band and was a stickler for proper recording technique:

And because Bob Sargeant had been the resident producer
of the John Peel [radio] show, he'd spent the last few years
with his engineers doing everything by the BBC book. Little
maps of the optimum angle for microphones to be set up,
and amplifiers to be valve amplifiers, and everything to be
immaculate, classic instruments, serviced to their zenith.
And we wanted to use whatever the new cheap synthesizer

was, or we wanted Japanese nose flutes; all the kids are getting them! No, no Japanese nose flute for the Beat. So everything was fairly organic. That means when you listen back to it now, it doesn't sound terribly out of date. A lot of the stuff that sounded thoroughly modern at the time now dates something to the point where it can often become unlistenable; it's so specific to its genre. And we avoided that. [xcii]

Ahead of the release of *Special Beat Service*, band members were worried. Local press in England had been mixed with the conventional wisdom being that the band's sound was out of fashion. Critics cited the release of the non-album single "Hit It" perhaps their quirkiest song as evidence. Funky and spastic like an art new wave Devo song, "Hit It" released in 1981 was an ode to masturbation that likely made radio DJs squeamish and was criticized for its poor sound mix. Roger hated the song:

It was one of the worst singles we put out. It sounded brash and harsh. Dave wrote the song about autoeroticism. I wasn't interested. It was one of the few Beat singles that I didn't like. [xciii]

After seven Top 30 hits in a row, "Hit It" languished at #70 on the UK charts. Critics used the release as evidence that the band were not reaching as wide an audience as they did two years earlier. The NME said it sounded like a *"hazy, befuddled, jumble of half-conceived ideas, a seven-minute shadow of the real Beat."* [xciv]

But "Hit It" served as the template for the experimentation that would soon be revealed by the release of the first single – "Save It For Later" in the UK on April 2, 1982. The song peaked at #47 on the UK single charts and spent just four weeks on the charts with the NME stating in their review of the song that the band had lost its *"former sing and zeal."* The song reached #106 on the Billboard charts in the US, but would quickly become a cult favorite of fans, critics and other musicians (more on this later.)

The band followed-up "Save It For Later" with the release of "Jeannette" on September 3, 1982. Though inventive and experimental, it's public reception can be summed up by a review in the *Harlow Star* which stated its opinion unequivocally:

> *The Beat should stop releasing inferior singles like Jeannette in their search for that elusive hit. Instead they should put out a track like I Confess, Sorry or Sole Salvation – songs with flair, imagination and adventure, songs that don't dwell in the shadow of the band's old hits but show*

positive signs of progression. Let the audience come to them.[xcv]

Taking the *Harlow Star's* advice, the band released "I Confess" as the third and final single in early December 1982. *The Lichfield Mercury* called the release: "The Beat's new bid to beat the flops":

> *It is a brilliant song and the production with stately, echoing piano chords over the intro makes for quite an epic feel. If there is any justice, it should break the Beat's run of flop singles. "I Confess" is the best song they have come up with for ages. [xcvi]*

Once the album was released, reviewers were able to absorb the whole album versus individual songs. *Smash Hits* -- the pop music bible for British youth, then regularly selling 500,000 copies per issue, gave the album a 9/10. This was about as positive as the British music press would be, given they had all moved on to hyping the war between fans of Duran Duran and Spandau Ballet and covering the growing popularity of Boy George and Culture Club.

> *Still bang on form, this LP contains a splendid mixture of styles and tempos, from dancing and toasting to slow love songs and even a Haircut One Hundred soundalike in "Sorry." Songs like "Sugar & Stress" and "Ackee 1-2-3" are*

even better than the excellent singles "Save It For Later"
and "Jeanette." A great album, I can say no more. [xcvii]

Sadly, it peaked at #54 on the UK charts after a short 3 week stay
and was buried in the 1982 Christmas rush of other album
releases. The band acknowledged that the new album's varied
sound was due to changing musical interests. For Roger, *Special
Beat Service* was an attempt to capture the many different
experiences that had influenced the band during years of touring:

We were on tour with the Clash, the Police, Talking Heads,
we had R.E.M. opening for us – there were so many
influences coming from so many different places, what we
wanted to do was have all the styles we loved crammed into
the same record. [xcviii]

Steele noted that he wasn't convinced that the new sound was the
right one yet:

It has changed in that we all had similar musical interests
when we first started, mainly punk and reggae, but now
everyone's into totally different stuff. That's why you get
different music from track to track on the new LP, and you'll
probably get an even wider variety of differences on the next
one. I still don't think we have the proper mix. We've always

been searching for the right sound, and I don't think we've found it yet. Maybe if we combine bits from all three LPs on the fourth one, we'll get something that's really good.[xcix]

Wakeling noted the band's collective uncertainty ahead of the album's October 1982 release in an interview with the band's local hometown newspaper: *We just didn't know what would happen. Half of us would be optimistic and the rest in the pits of depression – then we'd all swap round!* [c]

Morton shared his concerns about *Special Beat Service* with the band's *The Noise In This World* fanzine in 1982. He had a pointed message for the British record buying public – don't give up on us:

> *I know that there's new groups coming up all the time, but that doesn't mean the old groups are playing rubbish. Have a good listen, especially to the new album and if you don't like it, let it go. If you do like it, that's great. It could have been better maybe, but it's easy to say that when you've finished recording! It was the best we could do at that time and we put our heart into it.*[ci]

When asked ahead of the release of *Special Beat Service* what he thought 1983 held for the Beat, Wakleling responded with a prophetic sense that the band's time might be up:

Every time we finish an LP, I always think it's our last one,
and that's what I think now. However, by the New Year
when a few new songs have surfaced, I may feel ready for
the critical 4th album. On the other hand, maybe you should
start saving you're pennies 'cos you might have seven solo
LPs by next summer! Who can tell, isn't it exciting?! [cii]

In contrast to muted reviews in the UK, the critical response to
Special Beat Service in the US was generally positive from
American critics already in the band's corner, including the
Baltimore Sun pop music writer Geoffrey Himes who noted that
American soul was the main ingredient in this new musical
bouillabaisse:

> *Three years of playing together have paid off on the new*
> *album in a new sound that is so well unified that it sounds*
> *distinctively like the English Beat and no one else. The overt*
> *Caribbean and new wave influences have blended together*
> *around their common ancestor: American soul. The explicit*
> *political lyrics have been submerged into the love songs to*
> *produce insightful, emotional songs about power plays in the*
> *bedroom and kitchen.* [ciii]

J.D. Considine, writing for *Musician* in early 1983 agreed:

Unlike Wh'appen, Special Beat Service *successfully manages the transition from 2-Tone to full color, giving the English Beat a sound that is at once more soulful and harder rocking. Of course, that's basically what they were after in the first place, but where this new album succeeds is in managing that winning combination without succumbing to the limitations of a single style, the way ska did.*[civ]

Robert Chistgau of the *Village Voice* gave the album an A- and opined:

Career wise, a conservative move, Never has their four-four come on plainer, and when David Wakeling claims it's harder to write about the personal than the political, you're right to figure the songs will prove it. But David Steele can't resist a slight skank, and Everett Martin, who's such a pro he'd do Ringo imitations if they asked him, is also such a pro he can make any groove move. Anyway, Wakeling is always thoughtful about the irrational fear and real danger of letting go. The troubled decency of his modern romance, spilling over now and then into a barely discernible self-disgust, is the exact left-liberal equivalent of his social concern, of use to the great audience as well as the seekers after young lust and high infidelity he's aiming at.[cv]

More mainstream music press in the US offered mostly positive reviews. *Rolling Stone*, then the premiere music magazine in America, weighed in with an evenhanded review noting that the only band that could pull off such a "*broad range of musical idioms*" was the English Beat, saving praise for the "*hypnotically sluggish*" "Save It For Later" but also calling the album "*unassuming, heartwarming pop*":

> *Rather than stick to their original formula–a winning blend of ska, reggae, progressive politics and sheer adrenalin–the English Beat have elected to experiment with a broad range of musical idioms on their third album, and in so doing, they reveal the full range of their formidable talents.* Special Beat Service *sparkles with surprising touches that might sound incongruous were it not for the Beat's ability to make them sound perfectly right. Even when retracing their ska roots on "Jeanette" and "Sorry," they manage to incorporate, respectively, an Old-World accordion and snatches of Seventies Philadelphia funk. But the most striking departure is "Save It for Later," whose hypnotically sluggish melody, slashing rhythm guitars and manic viola infuse the Beat's customary tropical ambiance with more than a glimmer of the Velvet Underground's "White Light/White Heat."*

Apart from a few general homilies in "Sugar and Stress" to the effect that "this world is upside down," the English Beat have also foregone the topical verbiage of their earlier records. The Latin rhythms of "Ackee 1 2 3" end the album on a lighthearted note reminiscent of Haircut One Hundred. The English Beat may be more sophisticated and versatile than that band, but they seem to be playing music in much the same spirit these days. There's nothing on Special Beat Service *that's especially dazzling or profound; nonetheless, it eloquently demonstrates the creative possibilities of unassuming, heartwarming commercial pop.* [cvi]

The October 9, 1982 issue of *Billboard,* the weekly bible of the American music industry aimed at executives, talent buyers and sellers and retailers, published the following pithy but positive review:

This quick-footed British ensemble switches to I.R.S. with the digitally recorded album, which marks their most seductive melding of pop, rock and reggae yet. A multi-racial octet, they still allude directly to Jamaican ploys including elements of dub, but crisp production and increasingly deft playing point to the new rock market.[cvii]

So that's what the cream of the crop of American music press had to say about *Special Beat Service*. Here's my 17-year-old brain's track-by-track observations as best as I can remember all these years later. These reflections are augmented by anecdotes, stories and information that should help to put each song into context.

SPECIAL BEAT SERVICE - SIDE ONE

I distinctly remember getting home with the album and running up the stairs to my room and carefully removing the vinyl from the album sleeve and placing it gingerly on my turntable.

I CONFESS

I'm not sure what I was expecting but the first song on side one was definitely not it! My senses were hit with the melodic piano meditation of "I Confess," for four bars before Wakeling intones:

> Just out of spite
> I confess I've ruined three lives
> Now don't sleep so tight
> Because I didn't care till I found out that
> one of them was mine

Excuse me? The ska and reggae enthusiast in me was expecting something different and this wasn't it. As Stewart Mason succinctly noted in his retro review of "I Confess" for AllMusic:

> *What's with this Liberace-style piano intro? Why's it so mellow and mid-tempo, and why is there this vaguely Latin flavor to the rhythm section? And why is Dave Wakeling singing these sad, resigned lyrics about the end of a love affair instead of talking about how much Margaret Thatcher sucks?* [cviii]

But I quickly realized "I Confess" wasn't a throwaway love song. Instead of a ballad about everlasting love or unrequited love that cluttered early 80s pop radio, Wakeling had plunged the depths of his psyche for something altogether darker and emotionally harrowing. It might be fair to say that this is the same narrator of "Mirror In The Bathroom" who is older, but certainly not wiser. Instead of a song about self-obsession, this is a real time confession about ruining a relationship through infidelity, inattention and self-absorption.

Musically, the band had upped the ante by adding a string section and a Joe Jackson-inspired piano run by Wright that escalated the drama while Wakeling crooned and emoted. It's clear we are in uncharted territory sound and lyric wise. Wakeling had clearly had some romantic ups and downs since the release *of I Just Can't Stop It.*

What's also clear is that the band had created their own distinctive sound. It's not the dubby ska of their first record, and it's not the world beat inspired experimental reggae of their follow-up, but a winning combination of all their influences. But it takes a few spins before my teenaged ears get accustomed to this mature, upbeat Latin pop.

Though the song may not have set the pop charts on fire, it had an immediate impact on the band's musical contemporaries. During an interview published in the *New Music Express*, Elvis Costello, known to perform short bits of "Stand Down Margaret" during his live shows was quoted as saying he "loved" *Special Beat Service* and Wakeling's performance of "I Confess" in particular:

> *I love the Beat's new record, but it seems they're caught in a trap because everyone's saying, why isn't this about politics? But I think "I Confess" is one of the most beautiful bits of singing I've heard all year.* [cix]

Wakeling's wordplay on *Special Beat Service*, drew favorable comparisons to Costello from several music critics. As Wakeling noted: *I could have made it sound a lot more like Elvis than I did.*[cx]

But the comparisons to Costello should not have been surprising. Wakeling was a huge Costello fan and was inspired and influenced by his earlier recordings:

> *Right before I started in the Beat, I was working on a construction site. I had a ritual every day: Before I got on my motorbike to go to the site, I'd play "Welcome to the Working Week" as loud as my record player would do it. Hopefully, next door would bang against the wall, and that would make it sound even better to me. So he was a hero.*[cxi]

As I listened again and again to "I Confess" that afternoon, I was hypnotized. Wakeling's lyrics and vocal stylings gave me the same elusive warm feeling I've sought out from music since I was young. It seemed to capture – in dramatic fashion – the end of my parent's 22-year marriage. Further, in the video I created in my mind, it was my father, who did not share his feelings back then, lamenting the end of the marriage and the three lives in question were my mother, Wendy and me.

Little did I know that the origin of the song began with a piano lick that Wright shared with Wakeling. Before he was a member of the band, Wright worked as a social worker and then a truck driver. That's how he initially met the band:

I got a job for the day driving them down to London and back. We got on quite well, and that was it. And then they came around to see me and said they'd like me to be more involved. And they offered lighting director. It was nothing really with the gigs they were doing at that time which were so small there wasn't any lighting to speak of. Then, the whole band came around to see me one day, and asked, "Would I like to be the tour manager?" And I said, "Thank you." But I had no idea what that job was going to involve, except I'd worked with a few tour managers. And I tried to just copy what the best ones of them had been doing. This all took just a few months, and they soon signed the deal. After a few months they went into a studio to start recording the first album. And whilst they were halfway through doing that recording, they had three gigs to go and do.

It had been planned months before. They didn't want to do those gigs. They were interfering with the recording, but they had to be done for contractual reasons. And they said, "We are going to hire a keyboard and you're going to come and play with us." So I thought it was a joke. Didn't take it seriously until we got to the gig. They had got a keyboard on stage.

I remember the night really clearly. I remember thinking, "I'm going to be so low in the mix and as long as I get the intro to "Tears Of A Clown" right, then I'm okay here. That's the only thing I'm going to be heard doing anyway. Well, it was just fabulous fun. As all 2 Tone gigs did in those days, there was a huge stage invasion, 30 or 40 people on stage all leaping around like lunatics, slapping everybody on the back and all the rest of it, and doing no damage at all. And it was one of the most exhilarating things I've ever experienced. I was immediately asking, "Well, am I going to be a keyboard player or a tour manager?" Well, we opted for keyboard player. And then I didn't actually miss another gig between then and the end of the band. [cxii]

Once he became an established member of the band, Wright had a chance to be more creatively involved with the writing and recording of the *Special Beat Service* album. He soon collaborated with Wakeling on "I Confess." According to Wakeling:

One day I heard him playing a tune. I was like, "Ooh that's nice, what's that?" He said, "Oh, just this little calypso thing, I've had it in my head for ages." I was like, "It's fantastic, can you make a cassette of that?" It had all the charm of calypso, but the drama of Wuthering Heights, I thought, with the chord changes. David Steele came up with the bassline, which was very reminiscent of Chic. "Umm badumbam umm badumbam." Chic goes Calypso. The song started to form.

At the same time, I had a bit of an obsession with what was called "Photo Love" in England. They were those teen magazines where they had photographs with bubbles coming out of their mouths. Broken hearts and redemption, that sort of thing. I loved the cloying, hyper-driven emotion of them, and I'd had my photograph as a pin-up in a couple of them. I'd even talked my way, because of being a pop star, into actually acting in one. I got one where I was a prisoner who had just come out on parole, and my wife at the time got the part of my parole officer. Which was actually truer than anybody might have known, really. Very apt, I thought.

One thing led to another, and I started writing a song based on the emotional vibe of the magazines, mixed with the most sordid parts of my own experience that you could never really tell your best friends about. Once you're in the group, writing songs, you can mix in your real life with that sort of drama.[cxiii]

And just where did the nickname "Blockhead" come from? Wright explained that Saxa had nicknames for everyone in the band

(David Steele was "Shuffle" and a member of the road crew was "Smallhead") and that Saxa's nickname for him was a term of endearment because he was smart:

> *It was quite helpful to have the nickname. I mean there*
> *four Dave's around. There was me, there was Dave*
> *Wakeling, there was David Steele. And our main sound guy*
> *was called Dave Peters. So somebody would come into the*
> *dressing room and say, "Dave," and four heads would turn.*
> *So that had to change.*[cxiv]

Convinced of the marketability of "I Confess," I.R.S. tapped John "Jellybean" Benitez (known for making hits out of "Planet Rock" for Afrika Bambaata in 1982, "Let The Music Play" for Shannon in 1983 and his work with Madonna on "Holiday", "Lucky Star" and "Borderline" from her debut album) to remix a dance version of the song.

Benitez had become the go to remixer of choice in the early 80s after time spent as a DJ in dance clubs across New York City. Though his mix of "I Confess" did not sound distinctly different from the album version aside from the addition of extra congas and percussion, it was released as a separate 12" Maxi-Single. This approach fit neatly into the I.R.S. marketing strategy of reaching new fans on the dancefloor rather than Top 40 radio.

When I listen to the song now, it still packs an emotional punch and sounds timeless. In a 2022 retrospective review of the "100 Best Songs of 1982", the noted *Rolling Stone* music writer Rob Sheffield ranked "I Confess" at #71, sharing:

When you hear "I Confess" these days, it's uncanny how much it sounds like Taylor Swift wrote it, especially the extremely Tay climax where Wakeling yells, "My life's not open, please get out! I know I'm shouting! I like to shout!"[cxv]

JEANETTE

"Jeanette" came crashing out of the gate featuring accordion! Played by Jack Emblow, regarded as Britain's top jazz accordionist (he performed on the Beatles "All You Need Is Love" session in 1967), it added a wry musette feel married to the frantic and rhythmic beat provided by Steele and Morton. It was a complete departure from anything the band had previously recorded and reflected the go for broke approach they have adopted.

The lyrics featured more Costello-esque wordplay. I read and re-read the lyric sheet many times to make sure I could follow along with the quick rhyming narration about a one-night stand that captured the come on, the conquest and the hasty departure. It quickly became clear that neither party in the song was actually telling the truth about themselves and as the song unwound, it captured the awkwardness following the encounter: "*So we shared one last cigarette and swap false addresses.*" According to Wakeling, the "Jeanette" of the title was a composite of a certain type of girl:

> *It was an archetype, but there was somebody, evidently her name was Jeanette. It wasn't a friend of mine, but a friend of somebody else's in the group who did have a Ronettes' style haircut, like a big beehive hairdo. And she was the initial inspiration for the song. But then it sort of got written about an archetype, I suppose. Sort of a rich girl that might want to hang around musicians. Like a trustafarian or something.* [cxvi]

Roger's recollection on the origins of "Jeanette" were somewhat different than Wakeling's:

> *Jeanette was named after a girl Dave used to go out with who had a beehive hairdo and who worked at the dole office when we were signing on. Although I've heard Dave claim it's more of an archetype about a rich girl who likes to hang out with musicians. Either way, the accordion lent "Jeanette" a joyful French feel, even though it was a sad*

song. And the play on words and internal rhymes were very clever. [cxvii]

SORRY

The third song on side one "Sorry" captured my attention immediately. The song accelerated so quickly that a casual listener could miss the gravity of the story. It's a bleak tale packed into just two and a half minutes of mutated art rock meets Philly soul punctured by Magoogan's bleating horns, and Cox's hyperactive guitar picking.

Cox's guitar work on "Sorry" and across the album was probably his most rock oriented in particular. Cox explained his unique approach to playing guitar:

> *My sort of technical understanding of music is intuitive. The way I play in the band, although I do know the names of chords in an intellectual sort of way, I don't really think about it. Like the way we fit the band music together, we never talk about it, not the outcome. We might discuss arrangements or sections—someone might have a problem like "what chord is that?" and you tell them, but the way that he plays it is entirely up to him really.* [cxviii]

Across the band's first two albums Cox provided plenty of Jamaican music guitar rhythms, with the requisite damping and picking techniques which were informed by input from Roger:

> *If I didn't think the offbeat guitar sounded like proper reggae. I'd say, "This is how you do it. Dampen the chord like this." Small changes made a big difference. I saw myself as a vibes man.*[cxix]

But on *Special Beat Service,* Cox's soul side was revealed before it flourished in it's full glory on the Fine Young Cannibals debut. What I've always loved about his playing was that it was invariably supportive of the music and never remotely self-indulgent.

Wakeling was again at the top of his game lyrically as he listed the many real and perceived shortcomings of the man in question and the reasons, he must apologize to his woman, noting "*Words are just another violence. Nothing rings as true as silence.*" Roger added to the tension by echoing the chants of "sorry." The whole theme would normally lend itself to a slow country style ballad but instead is delivered in a fast stream of consciousness with jittery instrumentation that reflected the tenuous nature of the relationship. The reverbed horns and wailing Stax-like sax stabs raised the anxiety of the situation.

Later on after the release of the album, Wakeling confessed that the art funk of "Sorry" may have sounded a bit too much like Haircut 100, who were also a Bob Sargeant client:

> *Some people have compared parts of the new LP to Haircut 100, which is understandable because we share the same producer, Bob Sargeant. I do hear similarities, especially on 'Sorry', which I think sounds a bit too light. I think it would be a big mistake for us and Haircut 100 to start sounding too much alike, so whether we'll use Bob on the next LP is questionable.* [cxx]

Quick side note: Marc Fox, the percussionist for Haircut 100 played on *Special Beat Service* which may have been part of the cause for Wakeling's consternation!

The sound of the saxophone on "Sorry" and on nearly all of *Special Beat Service* was courtesy of new saxophone recruit Magoogan who was a well-respected studio musician. He had gained notoriety for an improvised sax solo he had played on Hazel O'Connor's song "Will You" which he had co-written with her and was featured on the soundtrack to the gritty 1980 new wave film *Breaking Glass* starring O'Connor as a young singer/songwriter. The soundtrack album reached number 5 in the UK charts and "Will You" was a UK Top 10.

While touring the UK in November and December 1980 in support of her album, O'Connor was supported by the then-unknown Duran Duran. In his autobiography, the band's bassist John Taylor stated that "Will You?" was "*the highlight*" of O'Connor's set, and called Magoogan's solo "*the emotional peak of the show.*"

Given the important role that Saxa had played in the band, filling his shoes should have been nearly impossible, but Magoogan was the right man for the job. He had started off by playing the clarinet as a boy and then attended the Royal Academy of Music for his training. Despite his classical musical education, Magoogan was self-taught on the saxophone and realized early on that he needed his own unique sound. Discovered by David Bowie's producer Tony Visconti playing in a London pub, it took him several years before he got his first break with multi-instrumentalist and solo artist Phil Cordell and the session guitarist Ray Fenwick who was a member of the Spencer Davis Group.

Magoogan joined the band after getting a call from his manager and went up to Birmingham to spend a few days with the band members and, most importantly to get Saxa's blessing. While the switch from Saxa to Magoogan could have been tricky given their different tones and playing styles, it was mostly seamless. Magoogan noted his impressions of Saxa upon meeting him:

I was first introduced to Saxa by Dave Wakeling in a Birmingham pub. Saxa was a lovely guy although somewhat of an enigma. He could appear to be crazy one minute and then the wisest man you could meet. He played from his soul and had a wonderful lilting lyrical way with his sax.[cxxi]

Wakeling was definitely a Magoogan fan and preferred his disciplined approach over Saxa's improvisational style:

You know where he's [Magoogan] going to come in, what he's going to play, and where he's going to stop, so I always know where I have to sing. Although Saxa is probably my biggest hero in the world, you never knew what he was going to do onstage. Whenever he felt like it was the end of a solo, he'd stop playing and I was supposed to start singing, even if it wasn't the right chord or verse.

It was magical having Saxa in the group. He was one of the cornerstones, and the idea of losing someone that important had us worried that the whole thing might fall apart. But it was amazing when Saxa and Wesley met because they just clicked. They were mates from the start. We were lucky the way it happened because it seemed very fraught at the time. It gives you a sort of faith in things."[cxxii]

Despite Magoogan's clear talent, Roger felt that *Special Beat Service* missed Saxa's touch. Roger's opinion was: *Wesley had a harsher sound which I didn't like for the Beat. It was never the same without Saxa.* [cxxiii]

Steele ended up missing Saxa for reasons more personal than musical, sharing: *He was a great old character, and not having him around makes the tour a lot less fun. He could always cheer me up onstage.*[cxxiv]

SOLE SALVATION

And then the skies opened up for me when I reached "Sole Salvation." That was the moment I fell deeply in love with *Special Beat Service.* The first few times I played the song it tugged at my heart in a way few songs had before. Despite its upbeat sound, there's something undeniably melancholy about "Sole Salvation" from start to finish. The song sounds like a punk soul take on Motown with the verses in minor chords that resolve into a more hopeful chorus based on a major progression of C-G-A. Even though I couldn't clearly understand all the lyrics that Wakeling crammed into three plus minutes of musical majesty, the feeling the track conveyed hit me immediately and still does.

Later on, as I graduated to making mix tapes for women I was dating, I would always include "Sole Salvation." It said everything my sensitive heart felt about romance and love along with ideas of tolerance and understanding. I also fervently believed that "Sole Salvation" was a potential hit. Instead, it was relegated to the B side of the single release of "I Confess."

The song kicks off with an insistent bass line that may be one of Steele's catchiest on the album and appears to take inspiration from the Jam's "Town Called Malice" which had a similar driving tone. The bass line was supported by Wright's organ chords and Morton's solid drumming which were augmented by rhythmic hand claps.

Here again Wakeling is highlighting the eternal personal and political battles that can lead to misunderstandings in everyday life and at the highest level of government. That said, Wakeling later shared in an interview with *Trouser Press* that a lot of his lyrics from the album were snippets "*gleaned from American soap operas and adverts,*" noting that his lyrics for Sole Salvation were influenced by Secret deodorant's well-known early 80s TV commercial tag line "*Strong enough for a man but made for a woman.*":

> Let's strike a brand-new deal
> That's strong enough for any man

But has a woman's understanding in it
And then finish!

Magoogan's baritone playing on "Sole Salvation" is sublime and his solo may be among his most heartfelt and memorable on the album. It dances and skips above the chords and melodies and the overall sound of the song is a further sneak peek at the Motown and soul influences that Steele and Cox would later explore in Fine Young Cannibals. No ska here, but that was fine with me. I could listen to Roger sing "Sole Salvation" as a backing vocal over and over.

The striking thing about "Sole Salvation" was that in the span of two years, the band had gone from covering a Motown song in a pop ska style – "Tears Of A Clown" to writing their own Motown-styled song. It further demonstrated how far they had come musically and how inventive they were. Much of this could be attributed to Steele's diverse and varied influences, as he explained to *Melody Maker* in 1980:

> *We're not a mod band. We're psychedelic calypso with soul undertones. I get my inspiration from bands like Genesis, who I hate. I don't want to be like them, so I write other stuff. I have different influences every week. Kraftwerk one week, the Four Tops the next, then the Monkees. Gary*

> *Glitter and the Monkees have been more of an influence*
> *than Prince Buster. And Wire. And the Shangri-Las.*[cxxv]

Wakeling shared during an interview with *Mother Jones* in 1985, shortly after the release of the first General Public album *All The Rage*, that the state of the world – both political and personal – inspired much of the material on *Special Beat Service* including "I Confess" and "Sole Salvation":

> *So, when people say, "Ah, it's just a load of love songs, isn't*
> *it?" I actually think some of them are much stronger*
> *political comments than what people seem to accept as being*
> *strong political comments. I think "Tenderness" on the*
> *current LP and "I Confess" and "Sole Salvation" on the last*
> *were every bit as strong a political comment as "Stand Down*
> *Margaret."* [cxxvi]

Quick side note: I've loved "Sole Salvation" so much that when my band Bigger Thomas were invited to be a part of a UK tribute album to the English Beat to raise money for teenage cancer, we recorded our own version of the song.

SPAR WID ME

After four emotionally complex songs, "Spar Wid Me," comes out of the blue as a respite and the band is joyfully back to playing reggae, but with a twist courtesy of Steele: a banjo on the intro and the choruses! As a full-on reggae head, even at 17, I was elated to finally hear what the band could bring to the table in comparison to their reggae bredren from Birmingham: UB40 and Steel Pulse. I wasn't disappointed.

"Spar Wid Me" was notable for putting Roger front and center. Though he was the spark plug of the band's live shows, he took more of a vocal support role to Wakeling on *Special Beat Service's* songs. But on "Spar Wid Me," his vocal stylings reflected the blues dances he grew up attending as a teen and gave Roger a chance to show off the MC skills he'd honed since he was nine years making up lyrics that he would chat over 70s dub records. From those early days, he made quick progress moving up from singing in the school choir to toasting with different Birmingham sound systems like Cyclops and Youthman Sound.

Though Roger might never be mentioned in the same sentence as the late 70s and early 80s Jamaican MCs he was inspired by -- Dennis Alcapone, Trinity, Dillinger, and Clint Eastwood, he was the perfect MC for an American pop audience who were completely unfamiliar with reggae and MC culture. Like his counterparts Neville Staple in the Specials and Astro in UB40, Roger successfully brought Jamaican influences into pop music.

Even his stage name – Ranking Roger which amused American
deejays, was an homage to the Jamaican toasters he looked up to:

> *I chose my nickname from school, "Ranking Roger", to DJ. It*
> *had a natural ring with two 'R's and sounded more*
> *showmanship than an alternative like "Jah Roger." DJs*
> *would prefix their names with "Jah" or "Ranking." There*
> *was Ranking Toyan and Ranking Joe. Ranking Dillinger*
> *was my hero.*[cxxvii]

Roger was likely inspired to write "Spar Wid Me" by the Jamaican
dancehall vocalist Ranking Toyan who released an album and
single titled *Spar With Me* in 1982 on the VP label which was
produced by Henry "Junjo" Lawes, then a leading Jamaican
producer and mixed by the dub producer Scientist. Roger's vocal
melody and chat cadence is very similar to Ranking Toyan's. For
many years I thought Roger's chat was a challenge for other MCs to
take him on in a sound clash. Instead, Roger – the self-professed
unity rocker, was looking to extend his hand in friendship,
understanding and love.

> *Spar Wid Me" was a track that I wrote for the third album.*
> *If someone is your "spa" they are your friend, and you move*
> *around together. It was the opposite of "spar" meaning "to*
> *fight." The song centered on the "one-drop", which naturally*

made it sound closer to UB40's style and sound. "Spar Wid Me" came out of a jam session. Shuffle [David Steele] said, "Here's one for you, a simple one," and played the bass line. cxxviii

The keyboard bubble on "Spar Wid Me" provided Wright with the opportunity to finally play authentic Jamaican style organ:

I wanted the organ to sound like it was recorded in Kingston. I wanted it to sound Jamaican. I wanted it to have that something. And I think it has. And I was so thrilled with it. cxxix

"Spar Wid Me" also featured another memorable saxophone solo from Magoogan playing ascending and descending runs that complement Roger's invitation to join the musical party.

ROTATING HEAD

Side one closes with "Rotating Head" and its sinister sounding Peter Gabriel-like new wave energy. It turned out that the menacing quality of the track was created by adding the sound of drill, circular saw and belt sander that Magoogan brought to the recording studio. According to Magoogan:

I recorded each tool for the duration of the song and then punched a rhythm out using the mute buttons on the mixing board. [cxxx]

The song also stands out musically because it features a Lyricon which was an unusual 80s era wind instrument. Invented by the Boston-based company Computone, it crossed a saxophone with an analog synthesizer and was famously heard on Michael Jackson's "Billie Jean" and Steely Dan's "Peg." The Lyricon worked by reacting to wind pressure (the harder you blew, the louder the sound), lip pressure (for pitch bend and vibrato) and to changes in pitch by fingering. The body of the instrument was modeled after the fingerings of the saxophone, with a few clarinet-like keys, and two octave keys.

On "Rotating Head" Magoogan's Lyricon creates an uneasy sound and his playing expertly conveys the sound of suspicion and mistrust amplified by the odd "*Ow, ow, ow*" sound effects created by running Magoogan's saxophone through a filter fitted on to the end of the bell of his instrument.

In addition to Magoogan's Lyricon playing, the lyrics to "Rotating Head" immediately caught my attention. As a kid who followed current events and politics, they were an abstract, short-hand recitation of what the early 80s and the height of the Cold War and nuclear paranoia sounded like to me. The song amplified the recent assassination attempt of Ronald Regan by John Hinkley Jr. a year and half earlier on March 30, 1981.

In the wake of the Reagan assassination attempt, the lyrics painted a composite of the surveillance mindset of Robocop-like agents deployed to serve and protect:

> Rotating heads, friends in high places
> No need to guess what he's got in that briefcase
> A mind like a gin-trap, one swollen ankle
> The rotating head tries to stay on the bright side of things
> On the right side of things

> Living on tiptoe
> Waiting for the next step
> The wages of death
> What a life for a swivelhead

> Understand, underhand, underarm protection
> Each new passer-by, a new wave of suspicion
> In less than an hour the plane will be leaving
> The lights and the cameras
> Then sleep on a prayer and a wing, rotating

As I listened and stared at the album cover, the concept of *Special Beat Service* made more sense. Perhaps it was a reference to the Secret Service agents who guarded American presidents, VIPs and dignitaries? I wasn't too far off. Wakeling shared that the lyrics were based on the experiences of and jargon used by bodyguards who had previously protected British Prime Minister Margaret Thatcher:

> *Get this, when the Beat got really famous, we had to have two bodyguards on the bus to get us in and out of the venues, but it turned out that both of them have worked as armed bodyguards for Margaret Thatcher. I sat at the front of the bus and talked their ears off. I gleaned a lot of their jargon from that, one being "swivelhead". They called themselves "swivelheads", and in the "Rotating Head" song, "friends in high places "means snipers on the roof, and "one swollen ankle" means someone has a pistol in a holster on the ankle. These were all things they'd say on the radio between each other. I also explained that tension and drama of life in that, and the trouble with getting to sleep at night when you may have to take a bullet [the] next day for Margaret Thatcher.* cxxxi

Just three years after the release of *Special Beat Service*, a remixed version of "Rotating Head" called "The March of the Swivelheads" –

a B side to "Jeanette" made a memorable appearance during the climactic scene near the end of the 1986 John Hughes film, *Ferris Bueller's Day Off.* In the scene, Matthew Broderick as Ferris Bueller is shown racing to get home before his sister.

Apparently, Hughes was an obsessive music fan who cemented the legacies of several artists – including the English Beat by building memorable film scenes around their songs:

> *The English Beat plays a crucial role in this coming-of-age classic, in which Matthew Broderick's Ferris Bueller famously commits truancy under the nose of his sister, Jeanie. After a series of misadventures involving faked illness, a parade float and a stolen Ferrari, Jeanie nearly hits Ferris with her car — and races him home. Cue up "March of the Swivelheads," an instrumental mix of horn-driven Special Beat Service deep cut "Rotating Head," as the perfect beat to this pulse-pounding adolescent moment.* [cxxxii]

Hughes told Wakeling he was a frustrated musician. As Wakeling recalled:

> *I spent quite a bit of time with him, went down to his house and hung out. He came to shows and we chatted backstage. He told me that's all he ever wanted to do*

actually, was be in a group. He was only making films because he never got to be in a group like he wanted. He had this amazing wall full of albums, and they were placed, not alphabetically, but in his own method of how he thought the music fitted together, and he made me quiz him. I'd have to tell him the name of a group, and he'd go straight to this whole length of a wall, four shelves high, with a little ladder with wheels. I'd say, "Tears for Fears," and he'd say, "Easy." I didn't catch him once; he knew where every record was. He was very nice. The first time I met him, he came into the dressing room in Orange County, California, and just walked straight up to me and shook hands and said, "Anybody who's got the balls to put a bassoon in a pop record is my kind of guy." That was his very first words to me. cxxxiii*

Wakeling explained how "Rotating Head" – a musical variation of "Mirror In The Bathroom" came about courtesy of a Dutch radio DJ:

The instrumental was first, and to be honest, had been derived from "Mirror in the Bathroom" backwards. There was a DJ in Amsterdam, that when you did his radio show, one of the things he thought was really cool was he gave you a cassette of your song backwards. And it sounded like

171

"Don't stop the marimba, Marmaduke", and it had a really good beat to it. It had a menacing sound to it. cxxxiv

It was Roger's idea that they use the backwards bass line as the basis for a new song. According to Roger

> *I said to Dave, "Listen to this. We could take the bass line and use it for a new song." Shuffle [David Steele] worked out the bass line in reverse and it became "Rotating Heads".* cxxxv

Wakeling explained the difference between the album song title and the instrumental title used in the film:

> *The instrumental was called "March of the Swivelheads" but "swivelheads" didn't really translate over here, and so "rotating head" fit better. The word swivelhead is in the song a couple of times, "What a life for a swivelhead." But rotating head fit better, sounded better, made a bit more sense in America, but still made sense in England, and it sounded a bit more like Talking Heads. A good extra bonus there.* cxxxvi

Let me use this interlude between side one and side two of the album to share some reflections on the musicianship of *Special Beat Service*. As a 17-year-old non-musician listening to the album I was more focused on the lyrics and the overall emotional impact the songs had on me. Later, as I became a musician, I was struck by the high level of musicianship particularly from each of the band members.

As a bass player, Steele has always been my north star. Early on, I modeled my playing style after how he played on *I Just Can't Stop It*. Many of the song's on the Bigger Thomas debut album released in 1989 are informed by his fast, driving repetitive style with lots of quick eighth notes and fifths off the root note. As I became more proficient I tended to gravitate more to his style of mixing reggae, pop, soul and punk as best as I could. And though his bass lines on *Special Beat Service* may not be as inventive or memorable as say "Mirror In The Bathroom" or "Twist And Crawl" from their debut, I'd argue that his playing on "Jeannette" and "Rotating Heads" come close to his distinctive and unorthodox approach.

Wakeling's guitar sound was also a defining factor. Most of the time he'd be tuned to open G and play high up the neck at the twelfth fret, which could sound like a higher-pitched, short-necked instrument. What he did was normally pretty simple, but he didn't sound like anyone else due to unusual tunings he employed (more details on this later).

Most of what Wright did on the keyboards was utilitarian and subtle, as a reggae or soul piano player should be, but there are flashes across side one of just how highly accomplished a musician he is and his time playing calypso in the West Indies is clearly an asset to the sound of the band.

Cox's guitar work is stellar though often overlooked. There are never any screaming leads, but plenty of reggae-styled rhythms featuring a lot of the damping and picking techniques he would have gleaned from early ska and rocksteady. What's clear from listening to side one is just how versatile a player Cox had become going from Latin rock to art funk to reggae to soul. If anything, side one of *Special Beat Service* celebrates the songs over individual performances, though there are many to relish.

But, for me, Morton is the MVP of the album. Like Cox, his versatility is astounding. I've always believed he didn't get the credit he deserved for helping to create such memorable music.

Need more proof? Just listen to his performance on "Twist And Crawl" from the band's debut. He's playing a sped-up rocksteady featuring eighth notes on the hi-hat with a quarter note accent while his kick pedal plays quarter notes and his rim shots play on the three, with a second rim shot on the four. Now compare that to syncopated Latin beat of "I Confess" and the steady, consistent Motown beat of "Sole Salvation." Like Cox, Morton's playing always served the song. And believe me, having known many drummers, self-control is not something many of them have! But the best do and Morton was one of the best.

SPECIAL BEAT SERVICE - SIDE TWO
SAVE IT FOR LATER

Side two of *Special Beat Service* opens with the album's centerpiece and touchstone. "Save It For Later" was unlike anything the band had ever played before. It's a simple, repeating three-chord pop song of D-A-G that floats on a bed of chiming rhythm guitar, churning cellos, and a buoyant sax solo. And despite the band's penchant for Jamaican sounds, the rock drone of the track came courtesy of Wakeling, who grew up listening to 60s rock.

> *In the late 60's to the early 70's, I was caught between the hippie and the skinhead movement. I had my hair cut so I didn't look like a straight at a hippie event, and I didn't look like a hippie at a skinhead event. It was a good haircut. I liked Van Morrison, Captain Beefheart, Tim Buckley, and skinhead reggae.*[cxxxvii]

"Save It For Later" was Wakeling's adolescent attempt to come to terms with the fact that he was expected to transition from boyhood to manhood. It's both a meditation on acceptance and a complaint about the everyday frustrations of growing up. I could relate. The lyrics "I *don't know how I'm meant to act with all of you lot/sometimes I don't try*" seemed particularly relevant to me as a 17-year-old. More poignantly, Wakeling had written "Save It For

Later" when he was roughly the same age that I was sitting in my room listening to it.

> *I wrote it when I was a teenager, before the Beat started. We did try it out the first few times in the Beat's rehearsals, but David Steele put the end to that; it was too "old-wave" for him. I don't know how or why, but he always considered he had a veto in the group. I mean, he was quite a bit of a genius as well, but he'd have had trouble sharing the stage with Mozart. It was about turning from a teenager to someone in their 20s, about not knowing what to do, because you knew people looked at you as though you were a man, but you knew you didn't know how to operate in a man's world. You still were responding to things the same way as you always had as a boy. It was about being lost, about not really knowing your role in the world, trying to find your place in the world, and you'd have all sorts of people telling you this, that, and the other, and advising you, and it didn't actually seem like they knew any better. So, it was like keep your advice to yourself. Save it – for later.* cxxxviii*

As a young man enduring one of the challenging periods in my life and trying to learn how to navigate the cruel world around me, the song spoke to me deeply. The line *"Cry, cry, but I don't need my mother/ Just hold my hand while I come / To a decision on it"* seemed tailor made to my current situation with the bullies at my school. I knew that I was the only one who could endure and overcome the situation. I needed to brave again and again, day after day, but it was taking a terrible toll on my soul and general well-being.

The unusual timbre of the song was due to the fact that when Wakeling wrote the song, he was playing his guitar upside down:

> *My dad gave me an acoustic guitar when I was 12, and neither of us knew how to play it. I was very confused by my posters of Jimi Hendrix and Paul McCartney. I thought that was the way you held it. So, for three years, I played the guitar – unbeknownst to me – upside down. I had no idea, but it seemed right to me. The hand on the fretboard with the funny shapes you have to make was difficult, whereas the other hand, strum, strum, strum— that seemed pretty easy, so I played with that one. I bought a Rolling Stones and a Beatles songbook. After two years, I gave up. I couldn't play a bloody thing. So, I tuned the guitar up to something that I thought sounded nice and just kept playing up and down with barre chords and added a finger here or there and created my own chords – so I thought. I had tuned my guitar to Keith Richards' "G" tuning that he used in the Rolling Stones. Once I realized that, all of a sudden, I could*

play Rolling Stones rock in the songbooks and that was good. I played most of the songs on the first album, and sometimes on the second and third album, with that tuning. There are some songs on the third album that are played with proper tuning. I tried to play along with John Martyn, and I couldn't. I tuned my guitar to what sounded about right on the John Martyn record, 'Solid Air'; and he used a tuning called BADGAD, which is in blues as well, but I tuned the G string up to an A, so it was all D's and A's. Someone told me that's a bagpipe tuning. I thought about writing my own songs on that tuning. 'Save it for Later' came out of that. One-finger wonder Wakeling. I wish I could be more scientific, but I would just tune the guitar until something sounded nice. [cxxxix]

"Save It For Later" also spoke to a young Roger the first time he heard it played and it prompted him to join the band:

If some songs were veering towards a world music sound, "Save It For Later" was more attributable to the rhythmic drone of The Velvet Underground. Dave wrote "Save It For Later" as a play on save it, fellator. The song dated back to Dave and Andy's time in the Isle of Wight. They used to play it at the Mercat Cross and it was one of the songs that made me want to be in the Beat in the first place. "Save It For

179

Later" sounded like a hit but in the nascent days of the band, Shuffle [David Steele] said it was "too rock...too old wave so it got dropped. cxl

When asked if "Save It For Later" was too slow a single release for a band who had built a reputation on playing fast dance tracks, Wakeling told the band's *Noise In This World* fanzine:

> *Coming up with a big wave of fashion, in our case 2 Tone, does mean that people expect a certain style, and (un)fortunately for us we have to keep trying different things to stop us from getting bored. What affects our decisions about singles? Shuffle [David Steele] says we always make good LPs and never release the right singles. Perhaps we're subconsciously so moral that we do it like that, so we don't get corrupted by lots of money.*cxli

The song had a profound effect on a young Adam Duritz, who later became the lead singer for the Counting Crows. Duritz, who is just a few months older than me, shared during an NPR interview in 2009 that "Save It For Later" was the perfect summer song. He had just graduated from Berkeley High School in the spring of 1983 when the band came to perform at the Greek Theatre and Duritz camped out all night to make sure he got tickets at the front of the stage. Like me, the song functioned as a piece of powerful nostalgia for him about a time when he was on the cusp of adulthood:

> *There's just something about the joy of the song. It just seems so technicolor to me. The harmonies and the melodies are perfect. There are so many interesting sounds going on. And I think that day is just so engraved in my memory. It was a beautiful, sunny, summer day. The sun had gone down, so the lights and the colors from the stage were lighting up as they came to play. And then the weird realization right afterwards that that was it. That was the end of the band. That was the last show they ever played. Those feelings that you don't get to hold on to. Those memories of a time you felt something about the music infused you with the celebration of it. It's funny because it's the only song I remember of the day. It's funny, because I'm picturing it in the sunlight, and I'm sure that they played it at night. It just seems like this crystalline, perfect summer day, and I'm just euphoric, and this song is just shimmering.* cxlii

Though most of us who fell in love with the song likely missed the sexual innuendo, what's more striking is the fact that the song almost wasn't recorded and its inclusion on *Special Beat Service* was tenuous until a showdown between Wakeling, backed by I.R.S and Steele. According to Wakeling:

The record company had liked it all along, but they didn't have any say in what songs went on the album. With the third record, though, David Steele really wanted a rest. He'd stopped writing hits on the third album—not the major ones, as it turned out. And the record company sort of had a hissy fit and said, "Well, fuck this, we've had this for long enough. This song's been a potential hit for the last three years, and you haven't written any hits this time out, David." At the same time, we'd managed to work some financial renegotiation with the label because something had not done as well as we'd thought, and in return, "Save It For Later" went on the record.

I never expected it would do so well, though I always liked the song before I was in the group. It's actually ended up earning about a third of our catalogue's publishing money, nowadays. Over the last 10 years or so, it counts for a full third of the catalogue. Very odd for a song that nearly never came out at all. It was only really when the record company insisted, and I got a bit of courage and said, "Well, look, if it's not on our record I'd just rather go and record it myself and bring it out." At that point David acquiesced.

It started off as a dirty schoolboy joke. The phrase "save it for later" is meant to be "save it," comma, "fellator." As in, "Leave it as it is, cocksucker." But we didn't have the term "cocksucker" in England at the time. We didn't really learn that one 'til we came to America. So it wasn't really a putdown, because we didn't really use that term to put down people at the time, and I don't think they do very much in England now, either. Anyways, that was the nature of the joke.

It was a song really about not knowing what to do, because you knew people looked at you as though you were a man, but you knew you didn't know how to operate in a man's world. You still were responding to things the same way as you always had as a boy. And it's a scary thing, really, being scared of all the implications of your life and not knowing what else to do other than to try and bravely march forward into the dark regardless. It's been hard to describe.

People ask, "What's that song about?" Well, it's about nothing. It's about not knowing anything. Or feeling like you know nothing and grasping in the dark for your place in the world and trying to do it with a wry humor. It's like your legs give way, and every time you try to stand up and pretend to be a man, the boy in you would flip over in front of everybody and you're embarrassed again, y'know? Particularly I suppose as you try and learn how to deal with girls turning into women. They could say one thing and you'd go bright red, look at the floor and start shuffling around like you just got told off by your teacher at school.

So that's what the song was about, and I'd written it on a National steel guitar I'd been given, and I was trying to find a tuning to play along to John Martyn's songs. It just sounded so hypnotic. I would play it for hour upon hour on this metal guitar. It would just be ringing, and I'd go a thousand miles away, and all these words and lyrics and images would start to pop into my head. Sometimes I'd just play it for an hour straight, and then stop and try it out with some lyrics.

After a long time, people were asking, "What is that thing you keep playing? It's very catchy, isn't it?" I was embarrassed they'd even heard it. It was for my ears only, as far as I was concerned at the time. And whilst I was going through it I was trying to think about those things about your transition from youth to manhood. [cxliii]

Ironically, for a song that changed the band's fortunes in America, most of the band, led by Steele, chose not to join Wakeling in recording it in the studio. The first take, aided by Sargeant, was just Wakeling and Morton:

> *We did try it out the first few times in the Beat's rehearsals, but David Steele put the end to that, and "End Of The Party" too, which I'd written just immediately prior to the Beat starting. Again, it was too "old-wave Dave" for him.*

> *So both of the songs were banned at first, and he even said some horrible things about them in interviews when they came out on the record, which I think was one of the other nails to the coffin for the Beat, really. Of that lineup, anyway. "Save It For Later" never got played until the third album, and then only at the record company's insistence, and even at that point David Steele still wouldn't play on the main track. "Oh, I'll do mine as an overdub, I'm not doing a backing track like that." And he didn't. Nor did anybody else, really. I knew the drummer would do it, so me and Everett played the song over and over until Bob Sargeant said we'd got a really good take on it, and then the rest of the band reluctantly acquiesced. And now I tease them rotten about the publishing earnings that they get from a song that they loathed.* [cxliv]

185

From just guitar and drums, the track grew to include strings which added a timeless quality to it. According to Wakeling:

> *We got a string quartet from the Royal Philharmonic Orchestra in London. They performed "Save It for Later" in their black-and-whites as if they were doing a concert at the Royal Festival Hall! They were serious professional classical musicians. Now the proof is in the pudding. The songs don't sound particularly dated and they don't sound as old as the songs that were trying to be terribly modern at the time. So we thank Bob for that. We didn't at the time.* [cxlv]

During recording, Wright was given the job of scoring the song which was one of the highlights of his time in the band:

> *I had a job to write out the score for the string parts as part of the recording of that. We have a string quartet in for the day to do the string part to Save It For Later. And I wrote the music for that. I was really proud of that.* [cxlvi]

The fantastic thing about "Save it For Later" is the surprises it springs around every corner. The little pithy sax riffs that come out of nowhere. The extra percussion that underscores the rock beat; the gorgeous string section; Roger's harmony vocals. Then there is the insistent repetition of "*now now now now now!*" And of course, during the coda while Wakeling is so moved that he's beyond words, there's Roger. At first, he's so quiet you strain to hear him. Then, his voice materializes in the ether of the melody, hovering like a ghost inside the world the song creates:

Runaway

Runaway

Runaway

Runaway

Runaway

Runaway

Runaway

And let me down

Because those harmonized "runaways" feel like they exist in a dream, every time I heard them, I wondered if I had really heard them. I'd go back and listen to the song again, just to verify that they were real. More than anything, "Save It For Later" documents a creative moment when the band blossomed as performers of the highest caliber. And, despite bandmember reluctance and in-fighting, the collective performance ultimately served the song.

As 'Save It For Later' became more popular after the end of the band, it took on a life of its own. Though Cox and Steele may not have been fans, the guitarist for the Who certainly was, and in the hands of Pete Townshend, the power of the song seemed to meet its destiny. Townshend may have been the right artist at the right time in his career to sing the song as it was written to be sung. According to the Locust Street blog:

> *Townshend was on stage at a charity gig in Brixton, and performed "Save it For Later," a recent hit from the Beat. Townshend sheared the song down to its skeleton, hanging the lyric on one repeated guitar figure. Singing in a harrowed but calm voice, Townshend lingers on the lyric's odd phrases infusing the line "your legs give way/you hit the ground" with weary resignation and taking the lyric's silly sex joke and turning it into a vulnerable plea.* [cxlvii]

Amazingly, Townshend had trouble learning the odd guitar tuning for the song and unexpectedly called Wakeling up on the phone to have him walk it through it.:

> *He phoned me up one morning and somebody gave me the phone and said it's Pete Townshend on a Saturday morning. And I sarcastically said, "Oh yes, he always phones about this time Saturdays." I thought to be honest it was Mickey Billingham from General Public at first because that's just the stunt Mickey would play that is. And so, I answered the phone in that light like, "Hello Pete ahaha." Then Pete*

replied, *"Oh hello Dave, err it's Peter Townshend here and I'm sitting with David Gilmour [Pink Floyd] and we're trying to work the chords to your song 'Save It For Later'."* Which was really, really weird because The Who's early singles and then 'Ummagumma' [Pink Floyd] had been two of the biggest sort of guitarist influences on me ever as I was growing up as well as Jimi Hendrix. It was stunning really, and it turned out I had made up the tuning to the song by accident.

So, I told them the source of my mistake and ingenuity, and they tuned their G's up to an A and that was it. He's done a few versions of it now, quite a number actually, but they are nearly always for charity, so I don't think I've made anything off of it as of yet! I must admit as he was telling me that him and David Gilmour were going to play my song, I thought wow, my heroes are going to play my song; this is going to pay me a fortune! And then he said oh this is for I think it was for an earthquake or a volcano benefit in Peru or Bolivia and I said, *"Oh no Pete, no, they've already had plenty of them over there they don't need any more!"* I don't know how funny he felt that was at the time. He's played it a lot of times, but I've only been ever paid in heavenly terms. It has never been earthbound by something as mundane as a fucking royalty! cxlviii

Townshend performed the song live for the first time with his backing band the Deep End at the Brixton Academy in November 1985. He introduced the song by saying:

> *There used to be a group called the Beat. A band I loved a lot. They did a song which I wanted to play tonight, and Dave Wakeling sent me the words and the tuning which is very interesting tuning. He said the Velvet Underground used to use it. It's a song called "Save It For Later." We're giving prizes afterwards for anyone who can tell me what it's about.* [cxlix]

The song soon became a regular staple of Townshend's live set and he released both studio and live versions of his rendition featuring his Deep End band which included Gilmour of Pink Floyd on guitar. If you've never heard Townshend's version, I urge you to put my book down right now and listen to it immediately. It might change your life and it might make you cry.

A few years later, Eddie Vedder brought the song "Better Man" to his Pearl Jam bandmates. The song – written when Vedder was a teen and performed with his first band Bad Radio is based on the same chords of "Save It For Later." Both songs are rooted in the key of D, and both songs utilize a simple I-V-IV progression for their respective choruses. Coincidently, the song was originally rejected by Vedder's bandmates when it was submitted for inclusion on *Vs.* but was finally recorded and released on *Vitalogy in 1994.*

Wakeling first heard "Better Man" while he was working for Greenpeace in the early 90s during a hiatus from music. He worked for the organization for close to five years and he led efforts to publicize the effects of global warming by using a solar generator-powered recording truck to record live concerts. Wakeling explained how he ended up working for Greenpeace:

> *When I was a teenager, I wanted to be in a group, or I wanted to work for Greenpeace, or I wanted to be a Buddhist monk. Those were the only three things I really wanted to do. I was doing some sort of soul searching in life. I had done a few Greenpeace benefit shows over the years, and a fellow in D.C. said if I ever fancied doing something for them, to give him a ring. So I phoned him. I ended up there five years. We got that Greenpeace table at concerts. We found a decent way to use celebrities, so instead of wheeling them in as star power, and they'd say the completely wrong thing in front of a bunch of cameras. So we talked to them about what they were really interested in and introduced them to campaigners, so they became more educated on the issues. In the early 90s, Greenpeace was having a really hard time getting any sort of hard news*

*coverage on global warming. It was like, well, "the science
isn't really in yet," or "it's too early to tell," things like that.
So we decided to record live concerts using a solar generator-
powered recording truck. We had solar panels on the roof,
and all these big, deep cell batteries that they'd used in an
Antarctic base that Greenpeace was dismantling. We made
it like a mobile exhibition room about global warming and
we used solar power to mix it, and when it was all done, we
took the generator to the cutting plant and we mastered a
CD.* [cl]

It was during his time with Greenpeace when Pearl Jam donated a
version of "Better Man" for the *Alternative NRG* compilation that
Wakeling produced that he noticed the similarities between the two
songs:

*They do a segue of it in 'Better Man' because it is, to be
honest, the same song and I found that out in the most
peculiar way. So we're recording the song in this really fancy
ranch place in Northern California and I'm looking at the
guitarist Stone Goddard and the line he's playing, and he
nods at me and I watch him again and he nods at me again
and then they took a break and he said, "Yeah, you're right
it's the same song," and I went, "What! I thought it might
be!"*

He said he used to work at 91X in San Diego as an intern
and that was his favorite song when he worked at the radio
station. So it is the same song and I think the association is
so nice that I've never bothered to chase any money on it
and they fit together perfectly so when I'm in Seattle I
always do a verse of 'Better Man' in the middle of 'Save it for
Later' to give them the honor back. [cli]

In honor of the English Beat, Pearl Jam regularly perform a live mash-up of "Better Man/Save It For Later" and it remains a fixture of their live set.

Sixteen years after its original release, "Save It For Later" was back on commercial radio and MTV in 1999 with a more modern version performed by the Seattle alternative rock band Harvey Danger who were best known for their song "Flagpole Sitta" from their impressive 1997 debut album, *Where Have All The Merrymakers Gone.*

I remember hearing the band's version of "Save It For Later" and being intrigued. It was an interesting and altogether unique take on the song and appeared on the soundtrack to the film *200 Cigarettes* which was produced and distributed by MTV. The plot of 200 Cigarettes followed a group of characters on New Year's Eve in New York City in 1981. The film received mostly negative reviews when it was released in February 1999 and was considered a flop.

That said, the song reached #29 on the Billboard Modern Rock chart and brought it to a whole new generation previously unfamiliar with the original. However, the Harvey Danger version has an interesting backstory. The band recorded multiple versions of "Save It For Later" for the movie soundtrack. The first had a backwards guitar solo that didn't quite work. The second version actually featured Mike McCready, the guitarist of Pearl Jam who recorded his "Better Man/Save It For Later" solo for the track.

According to the band's lead singer Sean Nelson:

> *MTV asked us to cover a song from 1981-82, but didn't specify which one, so we submitted ones by Devo, David Bowie, XTC and even Duran Duran; label demanded an English Beat song we all liked passively but not loved; later we found out the label was re-releasing the English Beat catalog in the US, a fact they neglected to divulge – one of the shadiest label manipulations we ever met.* [clii]

As a result, the band never performed the song live, until their last show in 2009.

In the summer of 2024, Eddie Vedder contributed a previously unreleased solo version of "Save It For Later" to the soundtrack of the critically acclaimed FX television series "The Bear." The song was used to great effect in a montage during Season 3 Episode 2:

> *It is used in an opening montage that takes viewers all across the show's setting of Chicago, with credits appearing over it. The scene shows various early morning routines taking place across the Windy City, including The Chicago Tribune being printed, bakers preparing various baked goods, a Zamboni clearing up an ice-skating rink, flowers being arranged, people kayaking in the Chicago River, and more. Some of the workers even smile at the camera. In some ways, this song is used as a love letter to the essential workers of Chicago, many of whom have been hard at work for hours while the rest of teeming masses are still dozing peacefully in their bedrooms.* [cliii]

Vedder's solo cut didn't take long to become a bestseller in the US. As of the writing of this book in July 2024, his version has reached #40 on the iTunes chart and was continuing to rise. And so, 42 years after its release in 1982, "Save It For Later" and the English Beat continue to tug at the heartstrings of viewers and listeners again.

SHE'S GOING

After the majesty of "Save It For Later," side two of the album segues into one of the band's quirkier and mysterious songs. "She's Going" brilliantly highlights how fantastically Wakeling and Roger's voices complement one another. Registering at just 130 seconds, "She's Going" is a dark tortured tale – set to an upbeat Calypso meets African Hi-Life sound about spousal abuse.

Again, due to Wakeling's clever wordplay, this only becomes apparent upon a close read of the lyrics. In this story, a woman is scared to leave her abusive partner but realizes nothing will change if she stays except, she may end up dead. She questions if her abuser will really miss her if she leaves but knows his apologies mean nothing and it dawns on him that he's missed a chance to convince her to stay: *"She found out that you don't give a damn/Just watch the spirit slipping out of her hand".*

Despite its brevity, it is technically complex. After a start in B major, the 1:00 mark brings an instrumental break which goes airborne at 1:17, before quickly shifting through several keys and then ending in E major for a frenetic closing verse and chorus.

According to Roger, the band was experimenting with musical styles and "She's Going" was one of those studio experiments:

Initially, we didn't know which way to go stylistically with the third album, but as we started to record the sound started to lean towards African influences. You can hear it on "She's Going." [cliv]

The heaviness of the song didn't really register with me until later in life when I read the lyrics very carefully. Wakeling and Roger sing the alternating lines so fast that the impact of the story is muted by the brevity of the song. Taking a closer look at the chorus, its much clearer that this is a do or die situation for the woman who has no choice but to leave and that the man in her life has run out of time to make amends:

> Like her prescription
> The drink tastes bitter
> As she turns round
> Found out that something hit her
> Would he notice?
> No never never never
> Would he miss her?
> She doesn't really care

"She's Going" is not a track the band played live, but it may be one of the most poignant and tragic songs about spousal abuse which is not a topic that was sung about during the new wave era of the late

70s and early 80s. Wakeling provided some insight into this idea of happy, danceable music with sad or painful lyrics:

> *We wanted happy music to show that life is a joy; it's a painful joy, of course, but it is a joy. But also, the stuff that goes on within our minds is often very, very painful, and I wanted that combination to happen in the same song, in the same three minutes. And I think that that's how it connected to people, because people's lives are complicated and often very painful. You know, life is a tragedy. It'll all end in tears, as the Buddha said. And so, anything you can do to try and pick people's spirits up, anything you can do to connect is a valuable aspiration, I think.* [clv]

PATO & ROGER AGO TALK

After two songs about the pain and complications of life, Roger returns with another upbeat slice of roots reggae with "Pato And Roger Ago Talk." Though he often shared vocal duties with Wakeling, his main role in the band was to "toast", and those toasts often contained the songs' most important emotional messages. And while the English Beat had consistently mixed elements of dub reggae with punk and soul, the band performed very few straight-ahead reggae songs. Though he was into all sorts of music, particularly punk, his first love and inspiration were reggae:

I used to practice in my bedroom all the time, making up

lyrics. I rewired a headphone as a microphone so I could

hear it through my speakers. At first, I would use other

people's lyrics and mix them with my own, like MCing over

"Good Times" by Chic, but mostly I practiced over reggae

records. The record that first inspired me to take up toasting

was African Dub All-Mighty Chapter 3 by Joe Gibbs & The

Professionals, who were the rhythm section Sly and Robbie.

I used to toast over a dub on that record all the time. clvi

My first question while listening to the song was "who is Pato

Banton?" It turns out, Banton was a 20-year-old MC then living in

Birmingham who caught the band's attention during a toasting

competition. The addition of Pato to the track gave Roger the

chance to become part of a deejay toasting duo, which was then all

the rage in Jamaica (see General Saint and Clint Eastwood and

their 1982 dancehall reggae smash hit "Another One Bites The

Dust"). Pato explained to me during a podcast interview I did with

him how he met Roger for the first time:

The English Beat was doing a performance at a theater on

the corner of my road, but before their performance, there

was a talent competition, and the winner of the talent

competition was promised the opportunity to work with

Roger in his recording studio. So, I turned up late to sign

199

into the talent competition and I had to beg the person at the front box office to please put my name at the end. And eventually they agreed. I waited until everybody else had performed and I went on stage and I started performing over my record. And then I decided to do some dancing because I was also one of the top dancers in Birmingham, so I did this dance move and I finished it with a high kick. But when I did the kick, I kicked the cable of the microphone and it broke and fell on the floor. And I was like, "oh my God I can't finish the lyric". But the music was still playing so I just danced off the stage.

When I danced off the stage, all the crowd started chanting, "we want more, we want more," but of course I couldn't do anymore because the mic was broken. Eventually they called me out and said, "you are the winner of the contest." I created such hype that I was named the winner. [clvii]

Roger related how Pato ended up on the track:

I like to claim that I discovered Pato Banton and gave him his first break in the music business. Pato won a toasting competition that I judged at the Imperial Cinema on the Moseley Road in Balsall Heath. The prize was 50 pounds, which was a lot of money back then. Pato was obviously the best toaster on the day, but I also thought he was far superior and more advanced than I was. He had the crowd in his power. He told funny stories about his family and did impressions of his mum. I said to him after, "Me and you will have to do something together." He was well up for it. The next time I saw the band, I said, "I've found this MC, I want to do something with him. He's a really nice guy." clviii

Pato and Roger wrote several songs together, but it was "Pato And Roger Ago Talk" that the band picked to record. Basing their style on original fast style toasters like U-Roy and I-Roy, Banton and Roger showcased their original take on speed and intricate rhymes. According to Roger:

The resulting "Pato And Roger Ago Talk" was a jam we originally recorded around the same time as "Hit It." "Ago" means "going to." General Saint and Clint Eastwood had just released "Tribute to General Echo", which combined their toasting, so the timing was really good for MC duos. We cut "Pato And Roger Ago Talk" as a solo record and issued it as a double A-side with "Cool Entertainer," credited to Ranking Roger as opposed to the Beat. The band talked me into having "Pato And Roger Ago Talk" on "Special Beat Service" and we used a version I mixed with Mike Hedges.
clix

The partnership between Roger and Pato was very fruitful and they established a friendship and working relationship that extended beyond the English Beat. Pato explained:

> *We actually became DJ partners for a while, working in his studio, writing lyrics and discussing music and the music industry. He was like my mentor as far as being a professional artist and the challenges of the music industry. And I was his street connection. I would keep him up to date of what was the most current style on the street and was happening with the British MCs and the new sounds. He would incorporate the ideas I would share with him into his music and then we'd record things. And he helped me produce one of my first singles as well, which became a hit in the UK.* [clx]

That hit song was "Hello Tosh" which Roger produced, and which went to number three on the British reggae charts. Pato credits the English Beat with helping to raise his profile across the UK. Banton repaid the favor for appearing on *Special Beat Service* when he invited Roger to join him on the raucous sequel "Pato and Roger Come Again" from his 1987 debut *Never Give In.*

SUGAR & STRESS

From the jaunty reggae of "Pato and Roger Ago Talk," the band pivoted with "Sugar and Stress," a manic new wave meets Sam & Dave styled track with ringing guitar and swelling horn lines. The song is the most overtly political on an album that avoided political commentary, but obliquely was likely aimed at the Reagan and Thatcher regimes then in power.

And while it's not on the level of earlier, overtly political songs like "Stand Down Margaret," or "Cheated" that had you thinking and moving your ass, "Sugar & Stress" has a timeless and clean 80s modern rock sound. More impressively, Wakeling's lyrics remain eerily prophetic more than 40 years later about the fractious and increasingly complex 21st century we live in where cable news and social media divides and isolates us from one another, culturally, politically and socially:

> These thought are so unfair
> If somethings there then it's worth taking.
> We know where our hearts are-right behind our wallets,
> Yes and that's where they're staying
> Grow up together but we grow apart
> Always climbing up is our downfall.
> A change of blood or a change of heart?
> Another change of address will do no good.

The song ends with the statement, "*I can't hang on for much longer*" which resonated with me completely as I hid out in my room that autumn of 1982 trying to escape the stress of my own life.

From a musical standpoint, the song is notable for what sounds like an acoustic guitar, Magoogan's incredible laughing sax solo, Stax-like horn stabs and a marked key modulation that occurs at the 1:57 mark of the song.

END OF THE PARTY

"End of the Party" has always been a personal favorite and the "could a been a contender" song that just wasn't given a chance to shine. The narrative follows a guy who appears to have ruined his chances in a relationship because he can't bring himself to commit or express his feelings. He thinks he can talk his way back to where it all went wrong. As the song unfolds, he realizes there is no going back, and he's missed his chance. The harmonies on the vocals are gorgeous and there's another can't-miss, should have been iconic sax solo from Saxa that, in my humble opinion, is better than Wham's "Careless Whisper".

"End Of The Party" is the only true love ballad the band ever recorded and it's comparable to other romantic ballads of the early 80s like "True" by Spandau Ballet, "Save A Prayer" by Duran

Duran, and the aforementioned "Careless Whisper" that were on constant rotation in the 80s. Sadly the moving lyrics also served as an epitaph for the band itself:

> You know there's never a next time
> How come the feeling that it's only just started
> Pull back your cover, I could love you for all time
> But do it now, you know there's never a next time

I've always believed that I.R.S. missed a huge opportunity for an American chart breakthrough by not issuing "End Of The Party" as a single. It could have been the band's big romantic track to compete with Joe Jackson's "Breaking Us In Two" which tread similar ground (melancholy, piano-based ballad) and reached number 18 on the Billboard Hot 100 chart in March 1983. I can attest, anecdotally, to the fact that nearly every woman I knew at college in the mid 80s loved the song and would have been the perfect audience for it's more tender side. Roger also thought it was a huge, missed opportunity.

> *"End Of The Party" should have been the last single. Amongst all the new romantic crap it would have gone BOOF! But Shuffle vetoed it; It would have smashed it. It had so much feeling: nice build, great saxophones; and it told a story. It was a great love song.* [clxi]

205

Wright considers the song an overlooked classic, particularly Saxa's solo that gives the song it's emotional punch:

> *There's something about Saxa's solo on "End of the Party." I can sing that note for note, the only other solos I can do like that, are some of the solos on Miles Davis' Kind of Blue album. But to me, Saxa's solo on "End of the Party" and the way that blends in with my piano, which is quite classical sounding is a magical thing. And I think Dave's vocals are fabulous at "End of the Party" as well.*[clxii]

I've always been surprised that no one has attempted a cover of "End Of The Party." Mark my words, that if an artist of some stature decides to perform it, they could have a hit on their hands.

ACKEE 1-2-3

And then, suddenly, we've reached the end of the album with "Ackee 1-2-3." An ackee is a tree indigenous to parts of West Africa and the Caribbean and known for its fruit which is edible as long as it's picked at the right time. Unripe ackee fruit contains a toxin which can cause death if it is eaten. Interestingly, ackee and salt fish is a popular dish in the Caribbean and is also the national dish of Jamaica.

But the band put a unique spin on the song with lyrics that make direct reference to a children's game exclusive to Birmingham. Ackee 1-2-3 was hide and seek with a Brummie twist:

People outside of the Midlands would probably give you a funny look if you yelled "Ackee 1 2 3!" at them.

The kid who was "It" closed their eyes and counted to 60 at a lamppost, tree or wall, and the rest went and hid. The boundaries of the hiding "zone" were always up for debate with the children who were always desperate to win.

"It" then went looking for you. If you were spotted, it was a dead sprint back to the safe zone, the place where the count began.

If you made it, you were safe. If "It" beat you back, they yelled "Ackee 1 2 3!" and your name, and you were out.

The first to get caught was "It" for the next round, and on and on it went until home time. Every group of kids had their own little "house rules" too, like being able to save someone else if they were the last one standing. [clxiii]

The song includes mentions of the various rules from the game –
the catcher who shouts "Ackee 1-2-3" when they find a runner who
then has to get back to the "den" before being tagged -- which serve
as metaphor for hiding from some uncomfortable truths. The song
also includes lyrics taken directly from the chorus of the King
Edward's School song, which happens to be the private school that
Wakeling attended as a boy:

> Forward where the knocks are hardest
>
> Some to failure some to fame
>
> Never mind the cheers or hooting
>
> Keep your head and play the game

The school song was traditionally sung at the end of the school year
by the entire student body who placed particular emphasis on the
final words of the first line of the chorus by always shouting
"SOME TO FAME!" It must have made an impression on Wakeling
who added it to his lyrics.

The song is loaded with pragmatic philosophical advice sung over a
rollicking and endearing calypso accompaniment. It takes on bias
and cruel judgments with the joyous refrain, "*Look we're all the
same it's only a game.*" The horns swing and the guitars bring the
song home as the last sounds of a dog barking bring the song and
the album to an end.

The studio recording was aided by the sound of Everett Morton's children who sang with Wakeling and Roger on the chorus. The song is a bittersweet farewell to *Special Beat Service* and prophetically to the end of the English Beat. According to Wakeling, the song was written when he needed to "*pull myself up off my sorry ass*" clxiv

When he introduced the song at the US Festival in 1983, Wakeling said, "*This one's all about, quite by surprise, catching yourself smiling. It don't happen very often, but when it happens, enjoy it! Ackee 1-2-3!*" The song served as the prefect pick me up for my 17-year-old sorry ass. It was a self-meditation I would say to myself as I prepared to head off to whatever trials and tribulations that the day had in store for me.

The song was released as a single in July 1983 instead of "End Of The Party" including another 12" remix by John "Jellybean" Benitez that gave the song some extra energy, but sadly flopped, stalling at number 54 in the UK charts. Roger was opposed to releasing the song:

> "*Ackee 1-2-3*" *was the kind of calypso music you heard in St. Lucia. It got drilled in my ears as a youth. I wanted reggae and punk and pop and things my parents probably hated.* clxv

While Roger may have disliked "Ackee 1-2-3" it was a song that I loved and played a lot. Without a male role model in my home, it surprisingly offered me sage advice about the power of positive thinking and how a smile could change your mood.

April 23, 1983

This world is upside down
The right's and wrong's
don't get much wronger.
Mistakes found in the past
Turn into rules protecting power.
It's falling down
It weighs a lot
So you should not depend on it.
This world is upside down
But look I can't hang on for much longer.

--Sugar and Stress

By Saturday, April 23, 1983 – the next time that the English Beat appeared on *American Bandstand* performing "I Confess" and "Save It For Later"—they were working their way across America with R.E.M. in tow as their support. I was watching from my usual spot in my bedroom, but even more excited because I had a ticket to see the band live the very next day!

During the break between songs, Dick Clark asked Wakeling, "*What's changed in your life since we last saw you?*" and Wakeling replied, "*We was on your show weren't we,*" and proceeded to share a story about being recognized in an American shopping mall and an odd anecdote about how their tour bus was attacked by frogs trying to cross from one side of a bridge to the other. Wakeling's

211

excitement and smile are genuine, so it's hard to tell in the moment that the grueling work of trying to break America will end the band in just a few months' time.

Steele looked on impassively during the Wakeling interview without saying a word (his steady glare spoke volumes!) Though never very voluble, he later explained his increasingly negative mindset about the state of the band in 1983 to *Spin* Magazine:

> *The classic mistake you can make in this business is to hate each other, release bad songs, and tour too much.*[clxvi]

Roger noted later that the signs and symptoms of an imminent split were apparent during the Spring of 1983:

> *By the time of Special Beat Service, we were so big in America. We were playing to twenty thousand people a night. Not getting any time off. It was gig after gig. We still hadn't had a hit and it seemed like everybody was saying to us, "How come you're selling out these enormous venues and you're not in the Top 10?" We were doing bigger, and bigger gigs and Dave and I were doing all the radio, TV and media interviews. Even though, within the band, we saw each other as equals, people saw Dave and I as the face of the*

> *Beat. That got to my head and believing that created a split*
> *in the band.* clxvii

Wakeling noted that some members of the band were less than enamored with the idea of breaking big in America and that sense of ambivalence was problematic:

> *We had become less of a success in England on the third*
> *album at exactly the same time as we finally broke in*
> *America and started to become a huge success there. And if*
> *the first thing wasn't bad enough to some of them, the*
> *second thing was a killer!* clxviii

During the fall of 1982 and winter and early spring of 1983, true to Jay Boberg's common sense approach, I.R.S. were pulling no punches in their marketing push. The sales arm of the label was shipping *Special Beat Service* merchandising aids like buttons, posters and album flats to retail chains around the US and encouraging customer contests and competitions.

The Strawberries record store chain co-promoted a "Special Beat Service to England" contest with Boston rock station WBCN and The Channel rock club. I.R.S also promoted the band's new songs by placing them on a variety of compilations, including the *I.R.S. Lost & Found* LP which featured 16 songs by I.R.S. bands including

R.E.M., the Go-Go's and the English Beat that had albums being released by the label.

This type of promotion had an impact and even without the benefit of radio play, the album moved close to 100,000 copies in the US which Steele attributed to "*the weird cult thing*" that surrounded the band in America. The other important factor was the rise of MTV as a way to reach the important youth market.

By early March 1983, the I.R.S. promotion machine had cranked to the ready and videos for "I Confess" and "Save It For Later" were shot, produced and getting regular airplay on MTV with the latter in medium rotation with 2-3 plays a day and the former in light rotation with 1-2 plays a day. Wakeling later noted that the videos for both songs were performance versus concept videos for a reason: MTV's rules and guidelines for videos:

> *Videos were really exciting before MTV. It was really exciting, and then when MTV started, they had some woman in an office over there with a rule book of thirty things you couldn't have in videos, like a censor. You had to send the rough cut to them, and she'd tell you which bits were allowed, and which were not, unless you were Madonna, and then you had to have all thirty of them. That was part of the game. And then it got really boring. From*

then on, we insisted on more performance-based videos than anything else. We had friends at home making really exciting three-minute films for $5,000, and they really moved you. Too much of a knee-jerk reaction by the record companies. Forty-year-olds thinking they know what fourteen-year-olds would be offended by, but of course most fourteen-year-olds aren't offended by anything. I thought it became very prurient, to be honest. It's no surprise to me that in the end, MTV ended up eating itself. [clxix]

Jane: Summer of 1983

It was at house party in March of 1983 that I first set eyes on Jane, a pretty and vivacious girl who attended a private school in Princeton. It was also the first time that I saw the video for "I Confess". I was immediately smitten with both.

One of Jane's classmates – who was in the Jewish youth group I had joined at the urging of my mother in the aftermath of my bullying experience, had talked me up to her saying, "I know boys from synagogue." Jane, who was not Jewish said, "Hey, as long as one of them has curly hair, I'm down." I'd never had a girlfriend and I hadn't dated anyone during all four years of high school. But that was all about to change.

The party was at Jane's parents' house about 20 minutes from Princeton. Her parents were away, and she had friends from her

*On the basement stairs in Jane's house
when we first met*

private school over. Jane and I first met on the steps leading down
to the basement. Our mutual friend was there to make the
introduction. Jane told me much later, *"I took one look, and it was
all over. I fell hard. It was a whole energy thing too.*

Jane had an infectious, friendly, upbeat vibe and a ready laugh.
She was a star lacrosse player at her school and also a talented
artist and photographer. She had striking eyes and I felt an
immediate connection with her. We became inseparable from that
night on. We quickly started talking on the phone nearly every
weeknight. On weekends I would drive down to her house, and we

would listen to music and watch MTV. Jane was just as music obsessed as I was and a huge fan of Madness, UB40 and the English Beat.

I sensed Jane's sensitive nature from the moment we met, and I opened up to her about what was going on in my personal life in a way I hadn't with anyone else before. Finally, after years of looking to music to help me sort through what had happened to me, I had a real person who listened to me and cared about me. Our connection blossomed and we embarked on what would become a sweet and wholesome romance based on genuine love and emotional support.

The noted German American psychologist Erik Erikson viewed crushes and youthful romances as important contributors to adolescent self-understanding and identity formation. He described teenage 'falling in love' as a form of self-development rather than true intimacy.

> *Adolescents, becoming more self-aware as their cognitive powers develop, can try out their 'grown-up' identities with romantic partners and through feedback from the partners' responses and behaviors, gradually clarify self-image. The endless talking that often accompanies teen romances is a way of experimenting with different forms of 'self' and testing their effect on the other person.*[clxx]

While some of that was true about my relationship with Jane, there was a certain level of maturity about our relationship which impressed those around us. We quickly became the nexus for our combined friend groups (my male friends and her female friends) and her house became our meeting place and summer base where we would meet before going out to movies, meals and most importantly, to see bands.

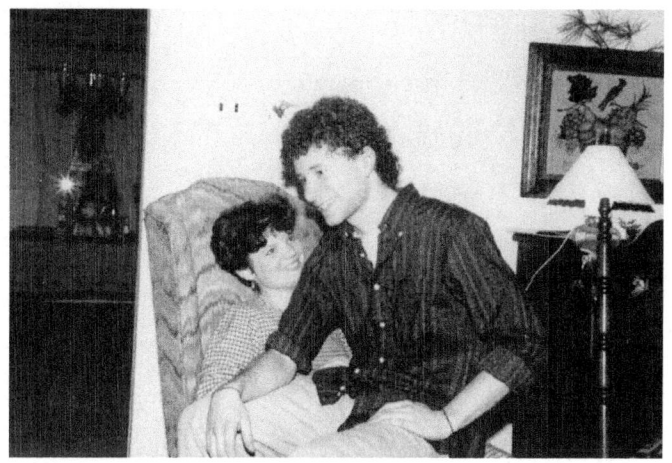

Jane's house the summer of 1983

Jane and I spent hours haunting record stores together and if either of us bought a new record we would go back to her house or my house and listen to it together. While I worked for a time at a David's Cookies store on Nassau Street in downtown Princeton across from Princeton University, Jane was working at Sesame Place just over the Delaware River from New Jersey in

Pennsylvania. After I lost my job slinging cookies, I would try to convince Jane to call in sick and come hang out with me, but she was dedicated to her summer job.

But more than anything, Jane was a safe harbor for me that summer of 1983. I think it was the first time I ever felt attracted to somebody physically and emotionally. I think I felt closer to Jane than I did to members of my own family that summer. And though Jane and I were physical, we were hot and heavy in a 1950s virginal sort of way. The fact that we never had sex – though we came close – kept the relationship pure and sweet.

At the same time, I was falling in love with Jane, I fell in love with the bass guitar. After some prodding, my mother agreed to order me a cheap, cherry-red bass guitar out of the Sears catalog. It arrived in a cardboard box and I stared at it for a few days in a complete panic. What was I supposed to do with this thing? When I slung it over my shoulder it was heavy, uncomfortable and awkward, and the metallic strings clanged when I plucked at them. I struggled to fret the notes with my fingers. It was a disaster. I felt defeated. It sat in a corner of my room for several months taunting me. It would be several years before I would pick it up again, though Jane encouraged me regularly to take lessons and learn how to play it.

While my relationship with Jane was blossoming that spring, my relationship with my father was deteriorating. I had become more assertive with him and often questioned him in what he called a "disrespectful tone." I just wanted answers to why things were the way they were, and he didn't have the patience or inclination to speak with me on that level. He did not consider us equals and did not take kindly to my growing impatience with him. We did not see each other much during this time. Looking back now, I realize how much I needed my father and how, with some maturity on my part and some flexibility on his, we could have been there for each other. Sadly, we remained estranged from each other for most the 80s and saw each other only sporadically.

This loss of a male role model was partially the reason that music from that Spring of 1983 is so memorable for me: it was an escape and I looked to it for guidance and advice. As Jane recalled to me later:

> *Well, music was always there for you. It was reliable, and that's the thing about music, especially when it's recorded. It's never going to change. You can always go back to it and it's always there. But I'm sure with your dad, you didn't really know what was coming next.*

As I spent more time at Jane's home, I became obsessive about watching MTV (her town had been wired for cable earlier than most in New Jersey). We spent many nights that hot summer sitting close to one another in her family's air-conditioned living room watching and waiting patiently for videos by our favorite bands to suddenly appear. And when an English Beat video suddenly appeared, it was ecstasy.

Mesmerized by MTV at Jane's House

Angst-riddled, gorgeous, and imminently watchable, the "I Confess" video directed by Mick Haggerty and C.D. Taylor immediately re-branded the English Beat as pin-up pop stars, with Wakeling and Roger getting the full-on matinee idol treatment. Haggerty was a real get, as he had directed many of the first memorable music videos for 80s artists including the Go Go's "Vacation" video, which was a 1983 Grammy Award nominee, and David Bowie's iconic "Let's Dance" video, which made him a star for a whole new generation of young fans like me. Haggerty would later direct videos for Simple Minds ("Alive and Kicking") and OMD ("The Pacific Age"). His co-director C.D. Taylor would later direct videos for both "Tenderness" and "Never You Done That" by Wakeling and Roger's post-English Beat band General Public.

Wakeling confirmed that the "I Confess" video – shot on a large sound stage in Los Angeles, was essentially making fun of new romantic bands like Spandau Ballet and Duran Duran who were then in heavy video rotation on MTV. But the beautifully shot video, with the band dressed in bright colors, and a focus on Wakeling's chiseled features, blonde hair and blue eyes, had the opposite effect. According to Wakeling:

> *And the video was a bit of a piss take on "The New Romantics," too. We were getting pretty jealous of them, y'know, because they'd stolen our thunder. We looked like a bunch of plumbers on the unemployment line in comparison. We were like, "Y'know, everybody goes through a phase of trying on their mum's clothes, and a little bit of makeup when she's out, but the idea is to get them back in the wardrobe and get your face washed before she gets home. You're not meant to go on TV like that, are you?" So we sort*

of camped it up a bit for that video, which was our mocking criticism, and that went completely over people's heads as well. We heard, "Oh, you look gorgeous!" Nooooo! [clxxi]

Wright shared that the video concept was misinterpreted:

It backfired because people thought he was trying to preen himself up to be like those guys. And he never tried to be like that or what not. [clxxii]

The video for "Save It For Later" – shot in England and directed by noted film director Julien Temple had a larger impact than "I Confess." The band, now light years away from their punky reggae roots, perform in what appears to be a 1950s Parisian, Beat-era club surrounded by indifferent artists and intellectuals who are ignoring their performance. After some prodding and cajoling from the band, the audience gradually join in and dance. Temple included several visual easter eggs including shots of several books from the Beat era and another where two women quickly glance at an eponymously titled 1960 album by French chanson singer Juliette Gréco.

According to Wright, the video was based on coffee bar culture that was popular in Britain in the late fifties and early sixties:

The video was shot in a sort of basement cellar place in London. I remember it smelled damp and horrible.[clxxiii]

Gaz Mayall – the son of the famous British Blues man John Mayall makes a cameo in the "Save It For Later" video and is hard to miss wearing his oversized fedora over a mop of black hair. Mayall gained notoriety as a DJ, singer, promoter producer, music historian and dandy. He hosted a regular weekly music night in Soho in London called Gaz's Rockin Blues that featured ska and reggae and was a magnet for many musicians including members of the Clash. It is likely that his weekly party served as part of the inspiration for the video.

By the spring of 1983, my life was in an altogether different place than it was during the band's first appearance on American Bandstand six months earlier. Though I sent applications to a number of colleges and had been rejected by most, I was accepted by Rutgers University which was just 30 minutes up the road from Princeton. Now that my college plans were sealed, I could finally try and enjoy my life as an 18-year-old. Jane had asked me to go to her school prom with her which helped to put a happy cap on the end of my senior year of high school.

Jane's High School Prom 1983

That said, my former friends turned bullies had filled out information cards for about 10-12 colleges during a college day at our high school, so every few days for a while that spring I received mail for Hymie Weiss at my home address. The sting and trauma of receiving these hateful reminders were ameliorated by the sudden emergence of Erik and Mark as friends I saw in school every day and then quickly outside of school as well.

Erik had arrived at our high school for his senior year to live with his mother after a year of living with his Father in Westchester, New York. He was culturally Jewish like me and quirky in a way that I found incredibly appealing. He had an off-kilter view of the world and a sardonic sense of humor that was the opposite of the edgy and mean-spirited WASPY boys I'd been hanging out. We became fast friends that year and spent a lot of time hanging out together after school talking. Erik also liked music, but more than anything, he was always up for doing something fun. He really was the key to getting me out of my shell that spring after all I had been through.

Mark was the youngest of six siblings and had moved to Princeton after his father took over as the CEO of a well-known company nearby. His family was welcoming and generous to Erik and me in a way I had never experienced before, and his home became a home away from home for us that spring and summer. His mother would often make us food to eat or put out snacks whenever we were there. As most of his older sisters were away at college, Mark had inherited their large record collections and was a music fan, particularly of Elvis Costello, Joe Jackson and Spit Enz. And so, Mark and I bonded over our shared love of music.

Erik, David, Mark and me (L to R)

Like Erik, he was a happy go lucky guy and ready to have fun in whatever form it took. It was through gentle prodding from Erik and Mark that I tried drinking and experimented with smoking weed for the first time. They delighted in my overly earnest reactions to being high for the first time and found it particularly hilarious when I went off on philosophical tangents about the music we were listening to while smoking!

As my relationships with Jane, Erik and Mark filled my life, my fortunes had also changed regarding transportation. My beloved grandfather (my mother's father) had suddenly passed away unexpectedly while out walking in his Sunnyside, Queens neighborhood that Spring of 1983. He had kept an olive green 1972

Plymouth Satellite – which Mark and Erik later affectionately dubbed "The Avocado" in pristine condition. Even though it was the size of a tank and drove like one, the car was his pride and joy, and upon his death, it was now mine. When I drove it home after his funeral, it still smelled of his aftershave. Though I was devastated that he had passed, the car was the greatest gift he could have given me. With a small boom box that played cassettes, the car became my rolling refuge, and a way to see my friends whenever I wanted.

The Avocado

More importantly, it allowed me to make the 30-minute trip up Route 1 from Princeton to a Ticketron outlet located inside a

Bamberger's at the Brunswick Square Mall on Route 18 in East Brunswick. During the early 80s, the Ticketron system used terminals called "electronic box offices" that were in publicly accessible locations, such as banks and department stores. Suddenly, the world of live music was now available to me. That spring and summer, Erik, Mark and I took many trips to the mall to purchase tickets for shows we would go and see including Elvis Costello, David Bowie and Madness.

One day that spring as I perused the back pages of the Village Voice for concert listings, I saw an ad for the English Beat at the Fountain Casino at the Jersey Shore. I immediately found Erik and Mark in school and convinced them we needed to cut our last period of school that day and head directly to East Brunswick. I stood mesmerized as a saleswoman from one of the make-up counters inside Bamberger's took our ticket order and a handful of our $1- and $5-dollar bills and then pushed a few buttons. Moments later these colorful blue, yellow and green tickets were printed. The saleswoman took the tickets, placed them inside a small white envelope, and handed them to me. I was finally going to see the English Beat!

April 24, 1983

The bees are busy
Now there's gold on the hill
The branches waving
But our hearts are wrapped up inside
And then you leave me so I start missing you a lot
No argument oh do I love you, I love you or not

--End Of The Party

As morning broke on Sunday April 24, 1983, I was up early, brimming with nervous energy. My first concert had been the Police and the Go Go's at Madison Square Garden on my 17th birthday in January 1982, but this show was going to be the first I would see at a real New Jersey rock club that was 19+ to get in.

The Fountain Casino was a modest sized Jersey shore rock club that had its heyday from 1981-1984 when popular bands including Joan Jett & the Blackhearts, Cheap Trick, Metallica, the Beach Boys, the Stray Cats, Twisted Sister and Alice Cooper played there. Into this mix of American rock and roll and heavy metal were sprinkled a few English new wave bands.

At the time, the drinking age in New Jersey was 19 years old -- soon to go up to 21. Since Erik, Mark and I were either 17 or 18 years old at the time, we took the necessary precaution of obtaining fake IDs at the Playland Video Arcade in Times Square in New York City. We caught the bus from Princeton into the Port Authority in Midtown Manhattan and then walked over to Playland which was nestled on Broadway between 42nd and 43rd Streets among single-room-occupancy hotels, massage parlors, greasy spoons, pornographic bookstores, X-rated movie theatres and peep shows. The area was bustling with hundreds of lost souls: down on their luck homeless people, sex workers and drug dealers, as well as street hustlers selling weed and chanting "smoke, smoke."

In 1983, Times Square was one of the seedier areas of New York City, but we were full of youthful hubris. Visiting was a necessary rite of passage undertaken by thousands of underage teenagers just like us looking for fake IDs that would gain them entry into clubs, bars and liquor stores. A story in the *New York Times* in 1986 reported on this phenomenon:

> *Youths from Manhattan are joined by their counterparts from Long Island, New Jersey and other suburban areas in buying what they see as a pass to bars, liquor stores and college fraternity parties. One Times Square merchant said he sold 100 to 150 of the laminated photo identification cards a day.*

Alan Chu, who lives in Chinatown, had just bought an identification card at a booth inside the Playland Arcade at 1485 Broadway, between 42d and 43d Streets, and said the man who had sold him the card realized that he was underage.

"The guy said, 'I'll bet you a hundred dollars you're not more than 13 years old,' " Mr. Chu said. "After I got it, I said: 'You would have lost. I'm 15 and a half.' " A man who sold the cards at the arcade said he had no comment on the boy's assertions.[clxxiv]

After handing over $10 each, Erik, Mark and I had our mug shots taken by a Playland employee, who then typed our names and fake birthdates on counterfeit Whitman College ID cards. We surmised that it would look more legitimate if we all had the same fake ID from the same fake college. When we tested our new IDs at a Times Square bar shortly afterwards, we were waved in by the bouncer. As we sipped on bottles of Budweiser, we enjoyed the taste of pending adulthood.

Unable to contain my excitement, I insisted to Erik and Mark that we leave for the venue on the early side. I'd never driven to the Jersey Shore on my own and in those days, before Google Maps and Waze, I wanted to give myself plenty of time to get there in case I got lost. I was nervous that our fake IDs might not work and didn't want to endure the embarrassment of being turned away at the door in front of a long line of other concertgoers. On the drive to the club, we played cassette tapes of each English Beat album on my boom box and shouted out the lyrics to our favorite songs.

After seeing the band perform in front of the bright shiny TV lights of *American Bandstand* the day before, the Fountain Casino seemed like the most unlikely place in America for the English Beat to be playing. The club was in the working-class enclave of Aberdeen, just off of the Garden State Parkway on a busy stretch of Route 35 dotted with strip malls, fast food joints and other dive bars.

We killed time in the large parking lot waiting for the doors to open and I openly fretted to Erik and Mark that we wouldn't get in. They good naturedly shrugged off my worries. Right on cue, the bouncers opened the doors and we dutifully lined up. The bouncers took our tickets, glanced at our fake IDs and waved us inside. My sense of relief was palpable, and Erik and Mark held their smiles and laughs until we were securely inside, teasing me for my worry.

Once my eyes acclimated to the dark light, I felt like Alice down the rabbit hole. We were surrounded by clusters of older adults in their 20s and 30s crowding the bar and chain-smoking cigarettes. The club, which held roughly 1,500 people, catered to a harder rock and metal crowd and some of the people were wearing leather jackets, metal t-shirts and long hair which added to my disorientation. I asked myself: "Could they also be fans of the English Beat?"

While Erik and Mark waited confidently at the bar for drinks, my eyes were drawn to the stage where I saw mic stands, amps and drums bathed in blinking reddish stage lights. I was overwhelmed by how close I was to finally see the band live with my own eyes. But more than anything, I felt oddly at home inside this smokey, dive bar of a club. I had a growing sense that my life was about to finally begin.

The opening act was R.E.M., who had just released *Murmur* on I.R.S. two weeks earlier on April 12, 1983. With great fanfare they were introduced by WPLJ-FM deejay Pat St. John and opened their set by playing "Moral Kiosk." I'd never heard of them, nor had most of the crowd who watched mostly in silence and clapped politely. It turned out that R.E.M. lead singer Michael Stipe was a fan of the English Beat and *I Just Can't Stop It.* It turned out that it's chiming, restless guitar sound was a major influence on R.E.M.'s early signature guitar sound.

After a month supporting Gang Of Four in September 1982 and then a string of headlining shows that fall, I.R.S. had added R.E.M as the support for the English Beat and Squeeze in front of 13,000 people at the Nassau Coliseum in Hempstead, NY that November. Having established a rapport with one another, R.E.M were tapped to play support on a run of 19 shows that spring of 1983. According to Michael Stipe:

> *Touring with the English Beat was exciting. We were playing places that were mostly all-age shows, and this is very hard to do. I think I can speak for all of us and say that we felt a certain camaraderie with them.*[clxxv]

I have to confess that I did not initially like R.E.M. Like most of the audience, I was primed for the headliners and the 30 minutes I had to listen to a band I was unfamiliar with was frustrating. Nevertheless, I watched them closely. Peter Buck was doing his best Pete Townshend impression, leaping around and windmilling his guitar in contrast to Stipe who stayed rooted to his mic stand flailing his arms while singing and moaning. It was only later that summer when I heard "Radio Free Europe" on college radio that I put two and two together and remembered I'd seen them live. I

soon became a big fan of them and their debut "Murmur." While I
may not have initially liked R.E.M., Roger loved them:

> *R.E.M were one of my favorite bands that opened for the*
> *Beat. I loved Peter Buck's guitar style. Every night half of*
> *the Beat would watch them play from the stage. If you're the*
> *support band and the main act is watching you, you're doing*
> *good, but they didn't think they were good. They were shy*
> *guys. Michael Stipe was always very nervous, and you*
> *would find him in a sweat before going on. I remember*
> *saying to him before one show, "Go out there and just do it*
> *because one day you guys are going to be massive." He didn't*
> *believe me. He'd say, "What! Us?" I could see the potential in*
> *R.E.M.* clxxvi

Wakeling was also a fan of R.E.M. and made a point of checking in
on them every night in the same way that Talking Heads had done
with the English Beat years earlier. Stipe wanted to know what
Wakeling thought of the support act:

> *He asked me what I thought of the group after about two or*
> *three shows, and I said, 'You've obviously got some really*
> *great songs, very evocative. But to be honest, I can't hear a*
> *bloody word you're singing. It's all mumbling. You need to*
> *enunciate, Michael, you need to get your words out there to*

the people. By the end of the tour, their first EP had sold about 10 million copies, and they were already much more famous than the English Beat would ever be. [clxxvii]

What is clear in retrospect from the show that night was that a palpable shift in alternative 80s music had begun. Though it wasn't apparent on the surface, the headliners were in the last throes of their pop life. In contrast, R.E.M. represented a new American indie rock that was beginning its ascent. While both acts were the offspring of what punk had birthed in the mid-'70s, the English Beat's ska-revival-to-pop-group arc had peaked. The end was just a few weeks away.

While the English Beat and all early British new wave music had dominated the early 80s and MTV up to that point, R.E.M. exemplified what was now happening on this side of the Atlantic, with a return to a more guitar/rock-based aesthetic. R.E.M., along with their UK counterparts the Smiths, were putting a tuneful, accessible and wholly irresistible spin on a re-engagement with guitar rock.

After what seemed like an excruciatingly long wait, the lights went down and suddenly the English Beat were standing in front of me. As WPLJ-FM radio deejay Pat St. John introduced them, the crowd surged towards the stage, and I was separated from Erik and Mark. I searched in vain for them over my shoulder during the first few chaotic seconds as smoke from the on-stage fog machine billowed across the crowd. Despite being surrounded by strangers, I settled in and did my best to focus on watching the band from where I stood stage left.

Without warning, the band kicked into a jaw dropping version of "Mirror In The Bathroom" and I began to have an out-of-body experience watching them. As the crowd undulated back and forth across the floor in response to the driving drum and bass energy and dueling guitars, I did my best to keep my balance while my senses were overwhelmed by the smell of sweat, cigarette smoke and stale beer. As the song ended on a dime, there was a deafening roar from the crowd and Roger said, "*Here's a slower one called "Doors Of Your Heart*," which gave the crowd a chance to reorient itself to the lilting reggae one drop rhythm and Wakeling and Roger's harmonies of "*I can feel love go bomp bomp*" of the chorus.

I paid very close attention to Wakeling and Roger in particular. I watched how they moved on stage, what they said between songs, and how they sang into their microphones. Cox was also a vision as

The English Beat at the Fountain Casino April 1983 (Joe Streno)

he knocked out guitar licks while doing a rubber legged dance around the stage. But it was the rhythm section of Steele and Morton that truly fascinated me. I was drawn to Steele's fingers on the fret board: they were a blur moving up and down as he shuffled and jerked his legs like a marionette on speed. I studied the interactions he had with the bare-chested Morton who was already covered in a coat of sweat that sprayed up when he hit his crash cymbals. I listened to how the bass and drums locked in, and how Morton's syncopated rim clicks meshed with Steele's bass lines to drive the songs forward. It was an education in stagecraft and performance that I have always tried to emulate in my own music.

Something mystical happened that night. The songs that had been a constant during the previous three years – serving as a soundtrack to many transitions and intense experiences, transported me spiritually. Though I did not shriek or yell during the show, I felt something shift inside me. Could this live concert be changing the trajectory of my life? Socio-cultural psychologists think so:

> *Beyond their daily uses, musical experiences might in effect have important roles to play in changing or transforming people's life path. Music is listened to by many in periods of transition, as solace, support or mirror, as means to maintain people who are gone, or to imagine some other fixtures. In addition, because musical experiences are complete human experiences, they might themselves trigger ruptures and transformations of people's lives.*[clxxviii]

As I watched the band, I was having a musical baptism. As sweat poured off me I felt cleansed by the experience. The smoke and flashing lights were part of a religious ritual that was exorcising the pain of the previous four years of my life. This live show became one of the most meaningful experiences of my life. I was on an emotional high for days afterwards.

Five years after this show, I was standing on a stage inside a large Rutgers University lecture hall about to play a sold-out benefit show. It was my very first show playing as a bass player in a ska and reggae band that I had started in the mold of the English Beat. As the show began, thoughts of that night at the Fountain Casino danced in my head.

Summer of 1983

She said to leave it till the end of the party
Do it now, you know there's never a next time
How come the feeling that it's only just started
Pull back your cover, I could love you for all time
But do it now, you know there's never a next time

--End Of The Party

Following their tour with R.E.M. the English Beat had the honor of being invited to perform at the sophomore edition of the US Festival held over Memorial Day weekend 1983 (and along with Oingo Biongo were the only two bands to play both US Festivals).

While much of the drama surrounding the festival had been focused on the Clash insisting that the festival organizers donate $100,000 to a local charity before they would perform, the English Beat and A Flock Of Seagulls reportedly got into a brief skirmish. It happened while the band were waiting behind a backstage screen for A Flock Of Seagulls to finish their set. According to Wakeling:

> *Something happened on stage during the Flock of Seagulls show that some of them weren't happy with, and voices got raised. And it kind of went on and got louder in Liverpool accents – it was like listening to the Beatles fight.*

We were about to go on stage soon, so we already had enough butterflies coming on. The last thing we needed was the sound of the Beatles arguing on the other side of the screen. And one member of [the English Beat] – I won't say who it was – thought it was actually a solid wall as opposed to a free-standing screen. So he kicked it and said, 'Shut up, you flock of fucking haircuts!,' thinking that he was just being insulting and that would get it off his chest. But at that point, the whole screen started falling and it hit the floor loudly. Then it was like West Side Story.

We're all facing up on each other. Most of us were really embarrassed, and a couple from the other side who wanted to fight anyway were willing to try and make something out of it. But better senses prevailed, and we were ushered away and they were ushered to the other end, and the screen was put back up and reality was restored [Laughs.]. We went on stage with extra verve.[clxxix]

The six months between US Festival appearances had tightened the band's sound and performance. According to Wakeling:

In '82, we'd been touring with the Clash, so I think we were in a punky/reggae mood. We'd been touring with the Police in '83, so that probably chilled us out for that one … the

Beat weren't going to do many gigs after that. So there was
a sense of [finality]. The '82 one is more energetic, but I
would say the '83 one is tighter and more choreographed.
clxxx

Following their appearance at the second US Festival, the band
learned that Arista had released their cover of the Andy Williams
classic "Can't Get Used To Losing You" from the *I Just Can't Stop*
It album as the lead single from the new compilation album *What*
Is Beat? The song becomes an unexpected hit, reaching #3 on the
UK charts. It would be the band's last song to reach the British
Top 40 and, ironically, they bookended their chart career on a high
note with another cover of a 60's classic.

Anecdotally, a similar ska version of the track had been recorded by
the Executive featuring future Wham members, George Michael
and Andrew Ridgely's short-lived 2 Tone ska band. The duo had
tried hawking a tape of it around to a few record labels, including
Go Feet but had no luck. Elvis Costello, who was a fan of the track,
had also hoped to cover it but later said, "*The Beat beat me to it a*
couple years later."clxxxi

According to Wright, the band had not been consulted by Arista
about the release of the greatest hits collection:

So we flew back from having done the US Festival, with "Can't Get Used To Losing You." having surprised everybody and gone up to number three in the chart. So we'd come back to England to go straight to the Top Of The Pops studio. clxxxii

During the band's very last Top Of The Pops appearance in May of 1983, Wakeling knew that the group was crumbling and decided to have some fun. While Roger strummed a guitar and Wright plucked at a harp to mimic the strings in the song, Wakeling took on the role of pop crooner. Watching the performance, no one would have known the band was in disarray, but Wakeling later shared that he was ready to leave:

*It was ironic that when we were ready to leave, the Beat had their first Top Three hit with "Can't Get Used To Losing You." I decided it was a hint from somewhere that we had to make a move. We were on TOTP and I took my jacket off at the end of the song, got off the stage and walked into the crowd whistling. That was my clue.*clxxxiii

As the record was falling back down the charts, Wakeling and Roger were secretly making plans to leave and start a new group. Then out of the blue, the band were invited to perform as support for the last three dates of David Bowie's Serious Moonlight

European Tour at the Milton Keynes Bowl on July 1-3, 1983. The dates were Bowie's first British dates in five years and they quickly sold out with close to 50,000 fans at each show. A BBC retrospective set the scene:

> *Alongside the die-hard Bowie fans, ska and reggae lovers had turned out to see support act The Beat, joining new romantics, punks and even a contingency of Hell's Angels, from memory. Bowie's new persona seemed to appeal to everyone, and it felt like half the country was there. The three dates, from 1 to 3 July, had been added to the end of the European leg of his Serious Moonlight tour, due to massive demand for tickets following the success of the Let's Dance album and its hit singles, including the title track.*[clxxxiv]

These three shows would be the last time the original members of the English Beat would ever perform together on stage. So it was bittersweet how many fans of the band showed up to the shows. Wright noted:

> *Even thought we were a support band, it was just incredible how many Beat t-shirts that were around the place. I mean, thousands. And we went down very, very well. So given that*

*that's where the band was at that precise moment, I think it
was two days after those three gigs with David Bowie that
Roger and Dave resigned.*[clxxxv]

Apparently on the first night of the shows, there was no Red Stripe
beer in the band's dressing room and Saxa, not recognizing Bowie
when he stopped by to check on the band, inadvertently scolded
him thinking he was a backstage production assistant. According to
Wakeling:

*David Bowie walks into our dressing room caravan, dressed
in short tuxedo, and asks if everything is alright, do we need
anything? Saxa says, 'Come with me sonny bwoy', puts his
arm around Bowie's shoulder and walks him to the fridge,
which he opens. 'Look in dere, you see any Red Stripe sonny
bwoy?' asks Saxa. 'No Saxa, you're right, there is none', says
David Bowie. Bowie leaves, comes back 15 minutes later
with 2 six packs of Red Stripe; Saxa is thrilled! Bowie
leaves, and Saxa says, 'Nice young man dat, who him to
come in our dressing room asking like dat?' I say, 'That's
David Bowie, Saxa'. Saxa says 'Bloodclaaat, a me a thought
he was a waiter!* [clxxxvi]

The episode of mistaken identification didn't deter Bowie from
inviting the band to join him on the next leg of the Serious

Moonlight tour. It turns out Bowie was a big fan of the band stating at one point:

> *A truly delicious sound! And stand-up guys to a man. We did some gigs together in '83 and it was just a treat to watch them in action.*[clxxxvii]

Unfortunately, due to deteriorating relations, the band didn't take Bowie up on his offer to tour. Steele and Cox had decided they wanted a two-year break from touring, while Wakeling and Roger had both become fathers and wanted to keep working and earning money. Roger noted that even though the shows with Bowie had been a success and despite his invitation to tour, the band was for all intents and purposes finished:

> *Bowie loved us so much he watched us – he was such a down to earth person. He was such a fan and even though we brought the house down we knew it was the last gig. Splitting up wasn't a black and white thing, it was a personality thing.*[clxxxviii]

Wakeling could see the writing on the wall and decided to write his letter of resignation two days after the Bowie gigs and left it under the door of the band's management office.

> *We were only just about bearing each other's company so*
> *two or three months with Bowie [in the US] was the*
> *absolute opposite of what they wanted. I look back and*
> *think, 'That was fucking stupid.' We should've just bought a*
> *bottle of Xanax and done it. We'd have been U2! Instead,*
> *Bowie took Kevin Rowland. And sent him packing after two*
> *weeks for being awkward.* clxxxix

Despite being blindsided by the abrupt nature of the way the band ended, Wright could see Wakeling's side of things:

> *I don't blame anybody for anything. It didn't just happen.*
> *There were reasons why. Dave [Wakeling] was right in*
> *thinking, what he thought. Wasn't he? I mean, he was right*
> *in thinking, "Well, they don't want do this. They don't want*
> *to do that. So what do they want to do?* cxc

Wakeling's perspective was that the band had run its course:

> *At the time, there wasn't much of an alternative. It wasn't*
> *such great bravery. A couple of the other lads wanted two*
> *years off, and were quite adamant about it, and we were*
> *trying to do a record deal with Virgin, who became aware of*
> *this. And they [bass player David Steele and guitarist Andy*
> *Cox] had good reason, they said it was 'more planes than*

buses' and just wanted to go shopping, not be recognised, buy some food, cook it and go back to bed, live a real life. They were worried we'd start writing songs about being on Rock 'n' Roll Boulevard, believing the lifestyle to the point it would become our reality and we'd be singing songs about it.

But me and Roger had just started having babies and the money up to that point had been split equally amongst the band, so everybody had done okay but nobody had really got enough to not do anything for a couple of years... so we didn't really have much option. It had been dying on the vine. You couldn't get anything done. What had been spontaneous and enthusiastic was now torturous and hard to do. [cxci]

Asked about the English Beat when the first Fine Young Cannibals' album was released, Cox and Steele had nothing positive to share. Cox told one writer:

It's sort of like we were ill with a really embarrassing disease, and now we're better and we don't like to discuss the symptoms. [cxcii]

Steele had his own dark analogy:

> *It's like if you went out with this dodgy girlfriend and then you see her three years later and think, 'My God, how did I go out with her?'* [cxciii]

Cox and Steele's sentiments were likely driven in part by a sense that fans and journalists were unaware of the key roles they had played in the band. Steele was annoyed that most fans and media assumed that he and Cox would struggle without Wakeling and Roger who were seen as the creative drivers of the band when in fact, it was the future Fine Young Cannibals who had written music for many of the band's most beloved songs. According to Steele:

> *Because when the Beat split up, people thought, 'Oh, they [Dave Wakeling and Ranking Roger] are going to go on and you guys are nothing.' I don't think it came out that we used to write a lot of the music, Andy and I — 'Mirror in the Bathroom,' 'Too Nice to Talk To,' most of the first LP. I think the only well-known song we didn't write was 'Save It for Later.'* [cxciv]

Once Wakeling and Roger officially announced their departure from the band, the remaining members initially planned to continue working together. Cox and Steele called into MTV, and producers at the fledgling network created an ad about their search for "a good vocalist who could affect you." Then available in 14 million homes across the US, the ad resulted in a deluge of over 1,000 audition tapes. According to Cox, the search lasted more than a year:

> *We got a lot of heavy metal singers. There aren't many good vocalists. That's why it was so difficult.*[cxcv]

Cox shared that the duo did find one singer from the ad, but he wasn't a good fit for a variety of reasons:

> *I listened to them (cassettes) before breakfast, but they were awful and it took us six to eight months to find someone, anyone and in that time we only found one person that we were interested in. Unfortunately, although this one person did have a lot of talent he didn't fit the profile of what we were looking for and in fact he was quite a bit older having already been in a doo-wop group back in the 1950s. Further complicating matters this contestant lived in New York and we were looking for someone on the other side of the Atlantic preferably.*[cxcvi]

The duo ultimately selected Roland Gift from the Hull-based ska band the Akrylykz who had supported the band on a UK tour. True to their word, two years after the dissolution of the English Beat in

1985, Fine Young Cannibals released their debut single, "Johnny Came Home", the first of five UK top-10 hits across the next four years. Two of their songs – "She Drives Me Crazy" and "Good Thing" from their "The Raw & The Cooked" album – later become US Billboard #1 hits in 1989.

As part of the launch of General Public, Wakeling discussed the breakdown of the band's complex interpersonal dynamics which ultimately lead to its demise during an interview with *Number One* Magazine:

> *The Beat wasn't set up for snap decisions and it wouldn't have worked if anybody had been in control. The Beat worked as a compromise, Two or three members would pull forward and four would pull against. There always used to be a veto in the Beat. We couldn't do anything unless all five of us agreed on it. It's much easier to say "No" than to say what you like. Sometimes if it meant you'd have to stay for an hour and rehearse, people in the Beat would rather say they didn't like it so they could go home for their tea. It got well comfy.*[cxcvii]

Roger later regretted the way that the band ended and lamented that the success Fine Young Cannibals enjoyed could have – under different circumstances been shared by all the original band members:

> *We then formed General Public (with former members of Dexys Midnight Runners) and I knew all along it was the wrong move – we would have been massive if we had stayed together. We would have come back to England and been bigger. Instead of that, the Fine Young Cannibals went on and did what the Beat should have done – but what's done is done.* cxcviii

Though General Public enjoyed moderate success in the US, with "Tenderness" which reached #27 on the Billboard charts in 1984, Wakeling understood the impact the English Beat and their songs had on fans like me as we confronted the miseries of life and the stoicism sometimes needed in the face of it:

> *But, I think after everything else, are the things that people say to you, no matter what mental state they're in, and have somebody tell you that one or two or three of your particular songs have cropped up time and time in their lives and the lyrics have been pertinent to the dramas or soap operas that they were going through and that those songs have helped them through those times either with a sense of irony or a sense of humor or even misery shared perhaps, is the most*

satisfying thing. Far more than any awards or places in rock history or whatever. For a songwriter the challenge is to write from your hearts and that you've touched other people's heart over the course of a century - I mean, you can't get finer than that. [cxcix]

Upon reflection, Wakeling later understood the impact the band had on other bands, musicians and their fans. When asked how he thought the English Beat would be remembered and what he would remember about the band he said:

I think it would be being everybody's favourite support band. Everybody wanted us to be the opening band, because we created a party for them to swim in to. And the list of bands, which I never guessed when I was fan at the Virgin Records shop – the Pretenders, Talking Heads, the Police, the Clash, David Bowie ... they all said we were the best opening band they ever had at the time.

The second one would be meeting people after shows, when they shake your hand, sometimes even calling you Mr. Wakeling, which was a bit worrying, because you think it's your Dad. You have to look over your shoulder! That would be weird, because he's been gone for ages.

But they just want to say, 'Thank you for everything you've given me'. And these are the people who've paid for everything you've eaten in the last 40 years ... and your kids and grandkids even. They get to meet you outside a show, with what hair they've got left stuck to their head, just wanting to thank you. cc

I distinctly remember learning about the break-up of the band during mid-July 1983. I was with Jane, Mark, and Erik and a group of friends and we were hanging out around a fountain on the campus of Princeton University. We overheard a few students mention that the band had called it quits. I didn't believe it and became upset.

I remember telling Jane I wanted to leave. She convinced me to stay and it wasn't until a few days later that the news was confirmed in a short news brief I read in *Rolling Stone*. I was devastated by the news. I felt like I had lost a close family friend. The only solace I found in my heartbreak was that Jane understood how sad I was and that she made me a mixed tape of songs that we both loved. Many of them were English Beat songs. She was one of the only people that truly understood how much the band and their music meant to me. Later, the blow was softened when I finally heard that Wakeling and Roger had a new project called General Public.

Summer of 1983

Jane later included her thoughts on our summer romance of 1983 that moved me years later when I read it. She more than anyone during that time in my life understood how important it was for me to try and love more in the moment:

> *I have learned that to live for the moment is what life is all about. Grab a moment, take a chance to show someone some love or a good time. To shed a tear in a dark late night no one will ever know, only God can turn that tear into a special moment sometime in the future. We are all equal, we*

will all die someday, therefore make life full of moments of
celebration.

But it only seems appropriate to give Wakeling the final word on
the wonder and mystery of our teen years during 1982 and 1983
and how those intense experiences made us who we are:

> *I was talking to Jerry Dammers about this, wondering what*
> *was it that made us at certain points in our teenage years*
> *decide we wanted to take a step back and start writing*
> *bloody poetry about it! For me, I think about the struggles I*
> *went through as a teenager, then how those struggles*
> *developed into my adult years, and it's the same kind of*
> *drive. Always looking, always searching for paradise, not*
> *being able to realise it's always right here, right now if you*
> *just stop and look properly.* [cci]

Epilogue

Make a cross
Make amends
Set the record straight
We've never said the only things we should have ever
Bothered saying
Lets write out a list of things we need
Lets strike a brand-new deal
That's strong enough for any man
But has a woman's understanding in it
And then finish!

-- Sole Salvation

I'm happy to report that I survived my late teen years, though it took time and therapy for me to really recover from the internalized trauma of my illness, my parents' divorce, and the anti-Semitic bullying I endured. Those experiences ultimately made me both more emotionally intelligent, intuitive, and sensitive which was a good thing but they also gave me a huge chip on my shoulder and a simmering anger that took me some time to resolve. But I'd like to think that music, and specifically 2 Tone and the English Beat in particular had a lot to do with my recovery and in molding me into the person I am now.

My father and I reconciled in the mid 1990s when he moved back to New Jersey. He's become one of the most important people in my life and we both made great effort to overcome what had initially torn us apart when my parents separated and divorced. He's my biggest fan and his pithy words of wisdom, about putting Super Glue in my toothpaste make much more sense to me now.

I also have the English Beat to thank for inspiring me to pursue music and for giving me the gumption to pick up a bass and start a band when I really didn't know how to play my instrument all that well. The fact is that my passion for the music and a desire to be in a band like the English Beat, was at times, all consuming. That desire really carried me and also informed the positive outlook I have that anything is possible if you put your mind to it.

The ska and reggae band that I started in 1988 – Bigger Thomas, set me on a path that has made the writing and performance of music a central part of my life since my early 20s. While being in a band – and I've been in a few, satisfied the need for music making, it ultimately has served as a way for me to build a surrogate family. I've known some of my bandmates for years and they are the brothers and sisters that I never had. My relationships with my many bandmates – aside from my immediate family members, have been some of the most important of my life. They have given what I do purpose and fellowship and fulfilled the love and respect I was so desperate for and that was missing for many years when I was younger.

Speaking of love, amazingly, Jane and I have stayed in touch throughout the years. Though we never rekindled the romance of that summer of 1983, and we are both happily married with families of our own, we have developed a long-distance friendship that has stood the test of time. Though months or years can pass between contact, when we connect, we pick up right where we left off. As always, she has always remained supportive of my musical and literary pursuits, and I have been supportive of and impressed by her ongoing artistic work.

I think the highlight of my musical life have been the few time that my bands played shows with members of the English Beat or I have come into contact with original members. In the early 90s, Bigger Thomas ended up opening several shows for the Special Beat – the band fronted by Ranking Roger and Neville Staple of the Specials which also featured Horace Panter and John Bradbury of the Specials. The chance to chat with and interact with all of them and to play in front of them really was extraordinary.

In fact, aside from the meeting with Dave Wakeling that I shared at the beginning of this book, it was meeting Ranking Roger during the summer of 1988 when he performed at City Gardens in

Trenton, New Jersey that also had an impact on my life as a musician. I went there with my now long-time bandmate Roger Apollon to see Ranking Roger and his band. As we entered the club, we saw Ranking Roger playing pinball. We stood watching him play and when he finished, he nodded at us and said hello. We started a conversation with him and explained that we had just started a ska band influenced by him and the English Beat. He was touched and asked us a few questions before wishing us luck and telling us to not give up and keep ska alive.

Fast forward three years to 1991 and Bigger Thomas were opening a show for the Special Beat at the Fast Lanes in Asbury Park, New Jersey. As our band was sitting in a cramped, damp and decrepit dressing room before we went on, there was a knock at the door. We opened it and there was Ranking Roger! He came in, sat down and spoke with us for 10 minutes or so. And as he spoke to us, he remembered me and Roger and said "*You took my advice. Congratulations!*"

Acknowledgments

I want to thank the following people for helping to bring this book to life:

All the members of the English Beat (Dave Wakeling, Ranking Roger, Andy Cox, David Steele, Everett Morton, Lionel Augustus "Saxa" Martin, Dave "Blockhead" Wright and Wesley Magoogan) who have inspired me in ways I can never fully thank them for.

Aimee for all her love and support and for encouraging me to share my own musician origin story. She is responsible for giving me the life and family I've always wanted.

Jane who loved me in a genuine and authentic way, shared my love of music and helped me through a very tough time in my life.

Mark and Erik who showed me what true friendship was and who helped to make 1983 one of the most memorable years of my life.

My father Marvin and my sister Wendy. I' loved being on this lifelong journey with both of you.

Adam Liebling for serving as an initial sounding board and for sharing great feedback with me on early versions of the book.

Charles Benoit for being another set of eyes and for great advice on how to add some important parts to the story.

Amy Yates Wuelfing and Steve DiLodovico for their ongoing support and for encouraging me to write another book.

Ebet Roberts for kindly allowing me to use her amazing photo of the band on the book cover.

Joe Streno for kindly sharing his photos of the English Beat from the Fountain Casino show we both attended in April 1983.

References

Preface

[i] The Beat: Twist & Crawl Malu Halasa pp 21, September 18, 1982

[ii] https://www.portlandmercury.com/portland/we-got-the-beat/Content?oid=1696632

[iii] https://thequietus.com/articles/14756-my-punk-the-english-beat-live-by-simon-price

[iv] https://www.rollingstone.com/music/music-lists/the-best-musical-discoveries-of-2011-22226/the-english-beat-special-beat-service-130563/

October 1, 1982

[v] https://www.thetvdb.com/series/american-bandstand/allseasons/official

[vi] The Beat: Twist & Crawl Malu Halasa p 29

[vii] https://louderthanwar.com/the-beat-whaappendemon-records-vinyl-release/

[viii] https://recordcollectormag.com/articles/beat

[ix] Stand, M. (1981) "The Beat Scene". The Face. The Beat.

[x] Lott, T. (1980) "The Beat: The Mad Hatters". Record Mirror. The Beat.

xi The Noise In This World fan club newsletter May 1981
https://issuu.com/superflake/docs/beat_zine_master/1

xii https://recordcollectormag.com/articles/beat

xiii The Beat: Twist & Crawl Malu Halasa pp 17-19

xiv The Noise In This World fan club newsletter May 1981
https://issuu.com/superflake/docs/beat_zine_master/1

xv Walls Come Tumbling Down Daniel Rachel p 271

xvi Smash Hits "A Career In Ranking" August 21-September 3, 1980 p 5-6

xvii https://www.udiscovermusic.com/news/everett-morton-drummer-of-the-beat-dies-at-71/

xviii Post Punk Diary: March 1980 George Gimarc p 23

xix Post Punk Diary: March 1980 George Gimarc p 23

xx Too Much Too Young – Rude Boys, Racism And The Soundtrack Of A Generation Daniel Rachel p 171

xxi https://www.birminghammail.co.uk/whats-on/music-nightlife-news/beat-that-ranking-roger-set-11831817

xxii The Noise In This World fan club newsletter May 1981
https://issuu.com/superflake/docs/beat_zine_master/1

xxiii Essentially Pop: Two-Tone Legend Dave Wakeling Talks To Essentially Pop 3/23/20 https://essentiallypop.com/epop/2020/03/two-tone-legend-dave-wakeling-talks-to-essentially-pop/

xxiv Walls Come Tumbling Down Daniel Rachel p 275

xxv https://writewyattuk.com/2018/04/20/back-with-a-special-beat-service-the-dave-wakeling-interview/

xxvi http://goldenageofmusicvideo.com/the-english-beatgeneral-publics-dave-wakeling-talks-about-the-complete-beat-box-set-teaching-pete-townshend-tuning-getting-scolded-by-elvis-costello-and-how-sting-got-that-t-shirt/

xxvii The Peel Sessions Ken Garner Random House p. 107

xxviii http://music-illuminati.com/interview-dave-wakeling

xxix https://www.songfacts.com/blog/interviews/dave-wakeling-of-the-english-beat

xxx https://www.abc.net.au/listen/doublej/music-reads/features/meet-the-man-who-got-fired-for-signing-radiohead/10266486

xxxi https://louderthanwar.com/the-beat-whaappendemon-records-vinyl-release/

xxxiihttps://issuu.com/superflake/docs/beat_zine_master/1?e=2254205/3670675

xxxiii IRS Special Beat Service Promo Article

xxxiv IRS Special Beat Service Promo Article

xxxv https://www.worldradiohistory.com/UK/Record-Mirror/80s/81/Record-Mirror-1981-05-09

xxxvi Trouser Press, Issue 64 August 1981 p 40

xxxvii Trouser Press, Issue 64 August 1981 p 40

xxxviii https://www.onamrecords.com/labels/i-r-s-records

xxxix https://itcamefromblog.com/2017/07/06/the-police-censored-in-their-prime/

xl KTRU, Rice Radio. The Beat interview 1982 https://scholarship.rice.edu/handle/1911/97307

xli Billboard November 13, 1982 IRS, A&M Staffs Join In Push for English Beat p.66

xlii Billboard August 14, Midwest Theme: Do It Yourself: Boberg's Speech Highlights Chi Music Exchange p.6

xliii https://www.portlandmercury.com/portland/we-got-the-beat/Content?oid=1696632

xliv https://twitter.com/TheEnglishBeat/status/1334267731072360448

xlv https://zani.co.uk/zani-music/item/338-dave-wakeling-the-beat-goes-on

[xlvi] https://www.spin.com/2023/05/us-festival-40th-anniversary-oral-history/

[xlvii] https://www.lamag.com/mag-features/steve-wozniak-us-fest/

[xlviii] I Just Can't Stop It: My Life In The Beat – Ranking Roger p 197

[xlix] Interview with David "Blockhead" Wright January 14, 2022

[l] Interview with David "Blockhead" Wright January 14, 2022

[li] Not For You: Pearl Jam And The Present Tense Ronen Givony Bloomsbury Academic 2021 p. 35

[lii] Interview with David "Blockhead" Wright January 14, 2022

[liii] The Beat: Twist & Crawl Malu Halasa p 71

[liv] The Beat: Twist & Crawl Mala Halasa p 73

[lv] Siren Song: My Life in Music – Seymour Stein *p 182*

[lvi] I Just Can't Stop It: My Life In The Beat – Ranking Roger p 139

[lvii] Interview with David "Blockhead" Wright January 14, 2022

[lviii] Interview with David "Blockhead" Wright January 14, 2022

[lix] The Noise In This World fan club newsletter May 1981 https://issuu.com/superflake/docs/beat_zine_master/1

lx Simmons, S. (1980) "Talking Heads and The Beat at the Greek Theater Los Angeles". Sounds. The Beat, Talking Heads.

lxi I Just Can't Stop It: My Life In The Beat – Ranking Roger p 141-142

lxii Interview with Rob Hyman February 3, 2018

lxiii Siren Song: My Life in Music – Seymour Stein p 217

lxiv I Just Can't Stop It: My Life In The Beat – Ranking Roger p 226-227

lxv Interview with David "Blockhead" Wright January 14, 2022

lxvi Interview with David "Blockhead" Wright January 14, 2022

lxvii https://pennyblackmusic.co.uk/Home/Details?id=26036

lxviii Interview with David "Blockhead" Wright January 14, 2022

lxix https://ultimateclassicrock.com/beat-drummer-everett-morton-dead

lxx The English Beat Complete Beat Liner Notes Alex Ogg p. 7

lxxi The English Beat Complete Beat Liner Notes Alex Ogg p. 7-8

lxxii https://essentiallypop.com/epop/2020/03/two-tone-legend-dave-wakeling-talks-to-essentially-pop/

lxxiii (https://www.songfacts.com/blog/interviews/dave-wakeling-of-the-english-beat)

lxxiv https://web.archive.org/web/20180114183952/https://www.fredperry.com/subculture/article-interview-ranking-roger-of-the-beat

lxxv Himes, G. (1982) "For English Beat, Dance Music is the Medium for Tolerance". *Baltimore Sun*. The Beat

lxxvi https://louderthanwar.com/the-beat-whaappendemon-records-vinyl-release/)

lxxvii https://www.robertchristgau.com/get_album.php?id=3595

lxxviii The Noise In This World fan club newsletter May 1981 https://issuu.com/superflake/docs/beat_zine_master/1

lxxix http://goldenageofmusicvideo.com/the-english-beatgeneral-publics-dave-wakeling-talks-about-the-complete-beat-box-set-teaching-pete-townshend-tuning-getting-scolded-by-elvis-costello-and-how-sting-got-that-t-shirt/

lxxx Rolling Stone Magazine #353 10/1/81

lxxxi https://thequietus.com/articles/09008-roger-ranking-dave-wakeling-the-beat-interview

lxxxii The Beat: Twist & Crawl Mala Halasa p 107

lxxxiii Cooper, M. (1981) "The Beat: Wha'ppen? (Go Feet) ****". *Record Mirror*. The Beat.

lxxxiv KTRU, Rice Radio. The Beat interview 1982 https://scholarship.rice.edu/handle/1911/97307

April 23, 1983

lxxxv Record Mirror October 2, 1982 p 26

lxxxvi I Just Can't Stop It: My Life In The Beat – Ranking Roger p181

lxxxvii The Beat Goes On Trouser Press Issue 80 December 1982 p27

lxxxviii Interview with David "Blockhead" Wright January 14, 2022

lxxxix The Complete Beat Liner Notes

xc https://www.goldminemag.com/articles/the-beat-goes-on-for-ranking-roger-dave-wakeling-and-company

xci Interview with David "Blockhead" Wright January 14, 2022

xcii https://www.goldminemag.com/articles/the-beat-goes-on-for-ranking-roger-dave-wakeling-and-company

xciii I Just Can't Stop It: My Life In The Beat – Ranking Roger p172

xciv I Just Can't Stop It: My Life In The Beat – Ranking Roger p173

xcv Harlow Star "If You Can't Join Em Have a Go – Beat Em" 10/28/82

xcvi Lichfield Mercury November 26, 1982
https://www.britishnewspaperarchive.co.uk/viewer/bl/0000379/19821126/2 42/0051

xcvii *Smash Hits*. 30 September – 14 October 1982. p. 25.

xcviii The Complete Beat liner notes

xcix Holdship, B. (1983) "The English Beat: 2-Tone Survivors Make a Joyful Noise". *Musician*. The Beat. Retrieved December 5, 2021, from http://www.rocksbackpages.com/Library/Article/the-english-beat-2-tone-survivors-make-a-joyful-noise

c Birmingham Evening Mail "Sighs of relief as The Beat goes on" 10/13/82

ci *The Noise In This World* Issue Number 9

cii *The Noise In This World* Issue Number 9

ciii Himes, G. (1982) "For English Beat, Dance Music is the Medium for Tolerance". *Baltimore Sun*.

civ Considine, J. (1983) "The English Beat: Special Beat Service (IRS)". Musician. The Beat.

cv Christgau, R. English Beat Consumer Guide Reviews Special Beat Service https://www.robertchristgau.com/get_artist.php?name=The+English+Beat

cvi http://www.rollingstone.com/artists/theenglishbeat/albums/album/126110/review/5941258/special_beat_service

cvii Billboard October 9, 1982 p. 60

cviii https://www.allmusic.com/song/i-confess-mt0044158720

cix
http://www.elviscostello.info/wiki/index.php/New_Musical_Express,_Octob
er_30,_1982

cx Holdship, B. (1983) "The English Beat: 2-Tone Survivors Make a Joyful
Noise". Musician. The Beat. Retrieved December 5, 2021, from
http://www.rocksbackpages.com/Library/Article/the-english-beat-2-tone-
survivors-make-a-joyful-noise

cxi Murphy, T. (2011) "Dave Wakeling of The English Beat on having a
social conscience and Elvis Costello. Westword
https://www.westword.com/music/dave-wakeling-of-the-english-beat-on-
having-a-social-conscience-and-elvis-costello-5700622?storyPage=2

cxii Interview with David "Blockhead" Wright January 14, 2022

cxiii AV Club Dave Wakeling on the short, successful, fractious career of
The English Beat; 7/24/12 Noel Murray

cxiv Interview with David "Blockhead" Wright January 14, 2022

cxv https://www.rollingstone.com/music/music-lists/best-songs-of-1982-
1234592830/

cxvi https://www.songfacts.com/blog/interviews/dave-wakeling-of-the-
english-beat

cxvii I Just Can't Stop It: My Life In The Beat – Ranking Roger p184

cxviii The Noise In This World fan club newsletter May 1981
https://issuu.com/superflake/docs/beat_zine_master/1

cxix I Just Can't Stop It: My Life In The Beat – Ranking Roger p158

cxx Holdship, B. (1983) "The English Beat: 2-Tone Survivors Make a Joyful Noise". *Musician*. The Beat. Retrieved December 5, 2021, from http://www.rocksbackpages.com/Library/Article/the-english-beat-2-tone-survivors-make-a-joyful-noise

cxxi Interview with Wesley Magoogan September 6, 2022

cxxii Holdship, B. (1983) "The English Beat: 2-Tone Survivors Make a Joyful Noise". *Musician*. The Beat. Retrieved December 5, 2021, from http://www.rocksbackpages.com/Library/Article/the-english-beat-2-tone-survivors-make-a-joyful-noise

cxxiii I Just Can't Stop It: My Life In The Beat – Ranking Roger p186

cxxiv Holdship, B. (1983) "The English Beat: 2-Tone Survivors Make a Joyful Noise". *Musician*. The Beat. Retrieved December 5, 2021, from http://www.rocksbackpages.com/Library/Article/the-english-beat-2-tone-survivors-make-a-joyful-noise

cxxv Williams, M. (1980) "The Beat: Rankin' to Riches". *Melody Maker*.

cxxvi Mother Jones Magazine "Dave Wakeling Goes Public" p. 51-53 February/March 1985

cxxvii I Just Can't Stop It: My Life In The Beat – Ranking Roger p52

cxxviii I Just Can't Stop It: My Life In The Beat – Ranking Roger p184

cxxix Interview with David "Blockhead" Wright January 14, 2022 cxxx Interview with Wesley Magoogan September 6, 2022

cxxxi http://goldenageofmusicvideo.com/the-english-beatgeneral-publics-dave-wakeling-talks-about-the-complete-beat-box-set-teaching-pete-townshend-tuning-getting-scolded-by-elvis-costello-and-how-sting-got-that-t-shirt/

cxxxii https://www.billboard.com/music/rock/ranking-roger-english-beat-best-soundtrack-moments-8504341/

cxxxiii https://consequence.net/2012/07/interview-dave-wakeling-of-the-english-beat-and-general-public/2/

cxxxiv (https://consequence.net/2012/07/interview-dave-wakeling-of-the-english-beat-and-general-public/2/

cxxxv I Just Can't Stop It: My Life In The Beat – Ranking Roger p184

cxxxvi https://consequence.net/2012/07/interview-dave-wakeling-of-the-english-beat-and-general-public/2/

cxxxvii https://www.azquotes.com/quote/1450995

cxxxviii http://thejukeboxrebel.wikidot.com/the-beat-special-beat-service

cxxxix https://pennyblackmusic.co.uk/Home/Details?id=26036

cxl I Just Can't Stop It: My Life In The Beat – Ranking Roger p182

cxli The Noise In This World fan club newsletter Issue Number 9 cxlii https://www.npr.org/templates/story/story.php?storyId=111495148

cxliii https://www.avclub.com/dave-wakeling-on-the-short-successful-fractious-caree-1798232527

cxliv https://www.avclub.com/dave-wakeling-on-the-short-successful-fractious-caree-1798232527

cxlv Orange County Register; Interview: Dave Wakeling Looks Back at the English Beat's legacy as reissues, live set, local gigs arrive; 9/27/12; George Paul

cxlvi Interview with David "Blockhead" Wright January 14, 2022

cxlvii http://inkhornterm.blogspot.com/2006/11/100-years-in-ten-jumps-1986-ivor.html

cxlviii https://essentiallypop.com/epop/2020/03/two-tone-legend-dave-wakeling-talks-to-essentially-pop/

cxlix https://www.youtube.com/watch?v=pQ0zMDJKkbg

cl https://www.motherjones.com/media/2008/04/dave-wakeling-englishman-socal/

cli https://essentiallypop.com/epop/2020/03/two-tone-legend-dave-wakeling-talks-to-essentially-pop/

clii I Want To Talk About Harvey Danger Covering Save It For Later https://www.youtube.com/watch?v=R4eOH8IxfDk

[cliii] https://decider.com/2024/06/27/save-it-for-later-eddie-vedder-the-bear-season-3-episode-2/

[cliv] I Just Can't Stop It: My Life In The Beat – Ranking Roger p181

[clv] https://consequence.net/2012/07/interview-dave-wakeling-of-the-english-beat-and-general-public/

[clvi] I Just Can't Stop It: My Life In The Beat – Ranking Roger p50-51

[clvii] Interview with Pato Banton January 14, 2022

[clviii] I Just Can't Stop It: My Life In The Beat – Ranking Roger p185

[clix] I Just Can't Stop It: My Life In The Beat – Ranking Roger p185

[clx] Interview with Pato Banton January 14, 2022

[clxi] I Just Can't Stop It: My Life In The Beat – Ranking Roger p217

[clxii] Interview with David "Blockhead" Wright January 14, 2022

[clxiii] https://www.birminghammail.co.uk/news/nostalgia/playground-games-brummie-kids-used-24579286

[clxiv] https://tellme.typepad.com/tellme/2009/06/dave-wakeling-day.html

[clxv] I Just Can't Stop It: My Life In The Beat – Ranking Roger p217

April 24, 1983

clxvi Fine Young Cannibals Spin April 1986 p74

clxvii I Just Can't Stop It: My Life In The Beat – Ranking Roger p205-206

clxviii https://www.goldminemag.com/articles/the-beat-goes-on-for-ranking-roger-dave-wakeling-and-company

clxix http://goldenageofmusicvideo.com/the-english-beatgeneral-publics-dave-wakeling-talks-about-the-complete-beat-box-set-teaching-pete-townshend-tuning-getting-scolded-by-elvis-costello-and-how-sting-got-that-t-shirt/

clxx https://thepsychologist.bps.org.uk/volume-29/july/teenagers-love

clxxi https://www.avclub.com/dave-wakeling-on-the-short-successful-fractious-caree-1798232527

clxxii Interview with David "Blockhead" Wright January 14, 2022

clxxiii Interview with David "Blockhead" Wright January 14, 2022

clxxiv https://www.nytimes.com/1986/09/10/nyregion/despite-law-fake-id-cards-appear-easy-to-get.html

clxxv R.E.M. Reveal The Story of R.E.M. Johnny Black Backbeat Books 2004 p.77

clxxvi I Just Can't Stop It: My Life In The Beat – Ranking Roger p204 clxxvii https://flagpole.com/music/music-features/2009/06/03/the-english-beat/

clxxviii Cultural Psychology of Musical Experience p. 33 by Sven Hroar Klempe and Jaan Valsiner | May 19, 2016

Summer of 1983

clxxix https://www.spin.com/2023/05/us-festival-40th-anniversary-oral-history/

clxxx https://www.ocregister.com/2012/09/28/dave-wakeling-looks-back-at-the-english-beats-legacy/

clxxxi Costello, Elvis (2016). Unfaithful Music & Disappearing Ink. New York: Blue Rider Press. P. 357

clxxxii Interview with David "Blockhead" Wright January 14, 2022

clxxxiii Number One "The Party Line: A Political Broadcast On Behalf of The General Public" 3/3/84

clxxxiv https://www.bbc.com/news/uk-england-beds-bucks-herts-65988402

clxxxv Interview with David "Blockhead" Wright January 14, 2022

clxxxvi http://englishbeat.net/the-beating-heart-of-bowie-is-rebel-music-ripdavidbowie/

clxxxvii http://englishbeat.net/the-beating-heart-of-bowie-is-rebel-music-ripdavidbowie/

clxxxviii https://www.birminghammail.co.uk/whats-on/music-nightlife-news/beat-that-ranking-roger-set-11831817

clxxxix https://recordcollectormag.com/articles/beat

cxc Interview with David "Blockhead" Wright January 14, 2022

cxci https://writewyattuk.com/2023/09/02/try-a-little-tenderness-revisiting-general-public-four-decades-on/

cxcii https://www.rollingstone.com/music/music-features/chewing-the-fat-with-fine-young-cannibals-48065/2/

cxciii https://www.rollingstone.com/music/music-features/chewing-the-fat-with-fine-young-cannibals-48065/2/

cxciv https://www.rollingstone.com/music/music-features/chewing-the-fat-with-fine-young-cannibals-48065/2/

cxcv Spin Magazine April 1986 p. 74

cxcvi https://www.youtube.com/watch?v=DyydKTsPVqA

cxcvii Number One "The Party Line: A Political Broadcast On Behalf of The General Public" 3/3/84

cxcviii https://www.birminghammail.co.uk/whats-on/music-nightlife-news/beat-that-ranking-roger-set-11831817

cxcix Dave Wakeling Interview 3/15/10 (http://www.concertlivewire.com/thebeatint.htm)

[cc] https://writewyattuk.com/2018/04/20/back-with-a-special-beat-service-the-dave-wakeling-interview

[cci] https://writewyattuk.com/2018/04/20/back-with-a-special-beat-service-the-dave-wakeling-interview/

Printed in Dunstable, United Kingdom